Silver Arrows

Acknowledgement

This book could not have been realized without the help
of the many enthusiasts who so generously gave of their time,
trust and advice.

Prof. Jürgen Hubbert	Max-Gerrit von Pein
Wolfgang H. Inhester	Ron Dennis
Ulrich Ray	Mario Illien
Dr. Josef Ernst	Norbert Haug
Horst Bader	Stefan Röhrig
Klaus Balle	Wolfgang Schattling
Florian Bolsinger	Maria Feifel
Gerhard Heidbrink	Norbert Herrlinger
Martin Köbler	Roland Hiemer
Alfred Langer	Harry Ruckaberle
Gerd Langer	Marcel Hofmayer
Axel Lengert	Volker Mayer
Christoph Morlok	Stan Peschel
Michael Plag	Helmut Pless
Daniel Reinhard	Dieter Quattlender
Eberhard Renz	Martin Sauter
Wolfgang Rolli	Gert Straub
Thomas Saalfrank	Gudrun Wallach
Klaus Seibold	Hans Wiesner

Alessandro Franzoni,
Granite Marmi Pietre SRL, Carrara

Asessorato Cultura e Turismo,
Forte dei Marmi

Tristar Auto, Massa

MERCEDES-BENZ

Silver Arrows

Photography
MARKUS BOLSINGER

Text
CLAUSPETER BECKER

DELIUS KLASING VERLAG

Die Deutsche Bibliothek – CIP-Einheitsaufnahme

Mercedes-Benz – Silver Arrows / Markus Bolsinger/
Clauspeter Becker. – 1. Aufl. – Bielefeld:
Delius Klasing, 2002
ISBN 3-7688-1377-0

First published
by Delius, Klasing & Co. KG, Bielefeld
ISBN 3-7688-1377-0

Project manager:
Edwin Baaske
Idea, concept and photography:
Markus Bolsinger
Text:
Clauspeter Becker
Editors:
Hans Schilder, Axel Lengert
Graphic design:
Atelier Manfred Wezel, Filderstadt
Artwork:
Recom GmbH, Ostfildern
Specialist laboratory:
Quality Baur, Filderstadt
Reproduction:
C + S Repro GmbH, Filderstadt
Printing:
Kunst- und Werbedruck,
Bad Oeynhausen
Printed in Germany 2002

All rights reserved. No part of this publication may be reproduced, transmitted or copied in any form or by any means, e.g. by hand or with the aid of electronic or mechanical systems, including photocopying, recording and use of retrieval systems, without the express permission of the publishers.

CONTENTS

FOREWORD
*Professor Jürgen Hubbert
Board of Management
Mercedes-Benz Passenger Cars*

The 1930s

PHOTOGRAPHS
Mercedes W25

PHOTOGRAPHS
Mercedes W125

THE ORIGIN OF THE SILVER ARROWS
*Chronicle of the first generation –
the 1930s*

PHOTOGRAPHS
Mercedes W154

PHOTOGRAPHS
Mercedes W165

DRIVERS OF THE 1930S
*Manfred von Brauchitsch
Rudolf Caracciola*

The 1950s

PHOTOGRAPHS
*Mercedes W196
"Streamlined"*

THE RETURN OF THE SILVER ARROWS
*Chronicle of the second generation –
the 1950s*

PHOTOGRAPHS
*Mercedes W196
"Monoposto"*

DRIVERS OF THE 1950S
Juan Manuel Fangio

The 1990s

PHOTOGRAPHS
McLaren-Mercedes

SILVER MAKES A COMEBACK
*Chronicle of the third generation –
the 1990s*

DRIVERS OF THE 1990S
*Mika Hakkinen
David Coulthard*

UNSUNG HEROES
Patrolling the pits

GP DRIVERS PAST AND PRESENT
*A list of all Mercedes-Benz Grand
Prix drivers*

THE HALLMARK OF SILVER
*Silver Arrows – the extended
family*

FACTS AND FIGURES
*Technical data relating to
Mercedes-Benz Grand Prix cars*

IN THE FRAME
Picture credits

EDITORIAL

The decision taken back in 1989, that Mercedes-Benz should once again pick up its great tradition in motor sport, was as important as it was correct. In a field of industry increasingly marked by competition, it had become necessary to redefine the Mercedes-Benz brand in a more youthful and dynamic way.

This meant simultaneously achieving a number of things: new products, greater efficiency and a persuasive image. A century of motor racing has served to enhance the company's image, so it was clear that our decision to get behind the growing enthusiasm for this sport would certainly be a step in the right direction.

But it was not going to be easy for Mercedes-Benz suddenly to repeat its successes of the thirties and fifties in the much more competitive scene of modern-day Formula One racing. For this reason a long-term strategy was adopted for the third generation of Silver Arrows, one which would unfold gradually, each element building on the last. The concept was developed with Norbert Haug, who since 1990 has headed motor sport activities at Mercedes-Benz.

The plan for the comeback had a broad base and was oriented towards our trademark three-pointed star. The first point stood for what was at the time still a distant goal: Formula One. The second pointed to the success already enjoyed by AMG in the German Touring Car championships (DTM). And the third point of the star showed the way towards Group C. With successes in long distance races, and Le Mans in particular, our co-operation with Peter Sauber enabled us to underline our proven ability as a manufacturer of sports cars. Once the sports cars had done their job and brought home a world title, Mercedes-Benz and its team of partners were able to concentrate on Formula One and the DTM, and in both of these disciplines we are working hard towards achieving our ultimate goal of returning to the world's elite. What we have invested over the years in terms of ideas, human resources and finance is recompensed in many more ways than just titles and trophies.

This intensive involvement with motor sport has left Mercedes-Benz looking in extremely good shape in this its third generation of Silver Arrows. The challenge to become World Champions has captured the imagination of the entire workforce. Everyone has worked hard to make the brand image shine even more brightly. Our model range is considerably younger, much more dynamic and comprehensive than it was ten years ago. And for Mercedes-Benz this has also brought the planned economic success.

Professor Jürgen Hubbert
Member of the Board of Management, Mercedes-Benz Passenger Cars

The Mercedes W25 played the part of giant-slayer among racing cars back in 1934. With its sleek engineering, it followed the new formula for Grand Prix racing cars, which permitted a top weight of 750 kilograms. The new regulation was designed to bring to an end the generation of powerful but overweight racing leviathans, among which could be numbered the Mercedes SSK "White Elephants", weighing in at two metric tons a piece. But pensioning off the elephants did not automatically bring to an end the escalation of output as the sport's lawmakers had intended. In fact, with the Mercedes W25, the thirst for power was only just beginning. Its successor was the W125 (below)

Despite its considerable output, this Mercedes W125 was grateful for a helping hand

W25

The old racing engines – in particular, their spark plugs – were rather irksome in the pre-electronic era. They turned their noses up at common-or-garden porcelain insulation, preferring instead an expensive sandwich of glow plates. Moreover, they boasted a hefty caliber with an 18-mm thread and were accustomed to a pre-race aperitif supplied by warm-up spark plugs. Changing these was always hot work

The 1930s | 15

In the Mercedes W125 the 8-cylinder racing engine reached its peak. With over 600 hp by late 1937, it had almost doubled its output over early 1934

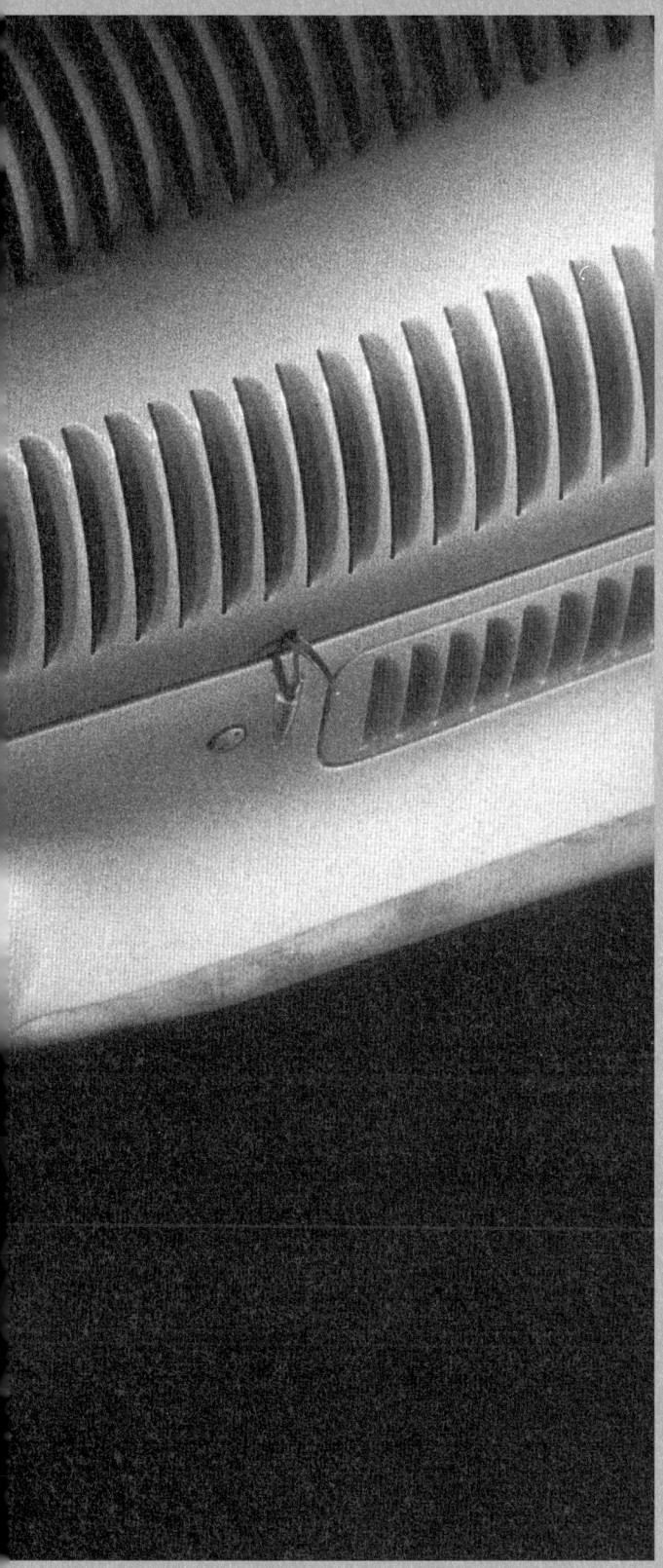

With the Mercedes W125, body design departed from the original functionality of the W25 and took on instead a new and efficient elegance. But mechanical construction, too, began to follow this approach. Under the overall command of Rudolf Uhlenhaut, modifications to the running gear improved suppleness and efficiency

W125

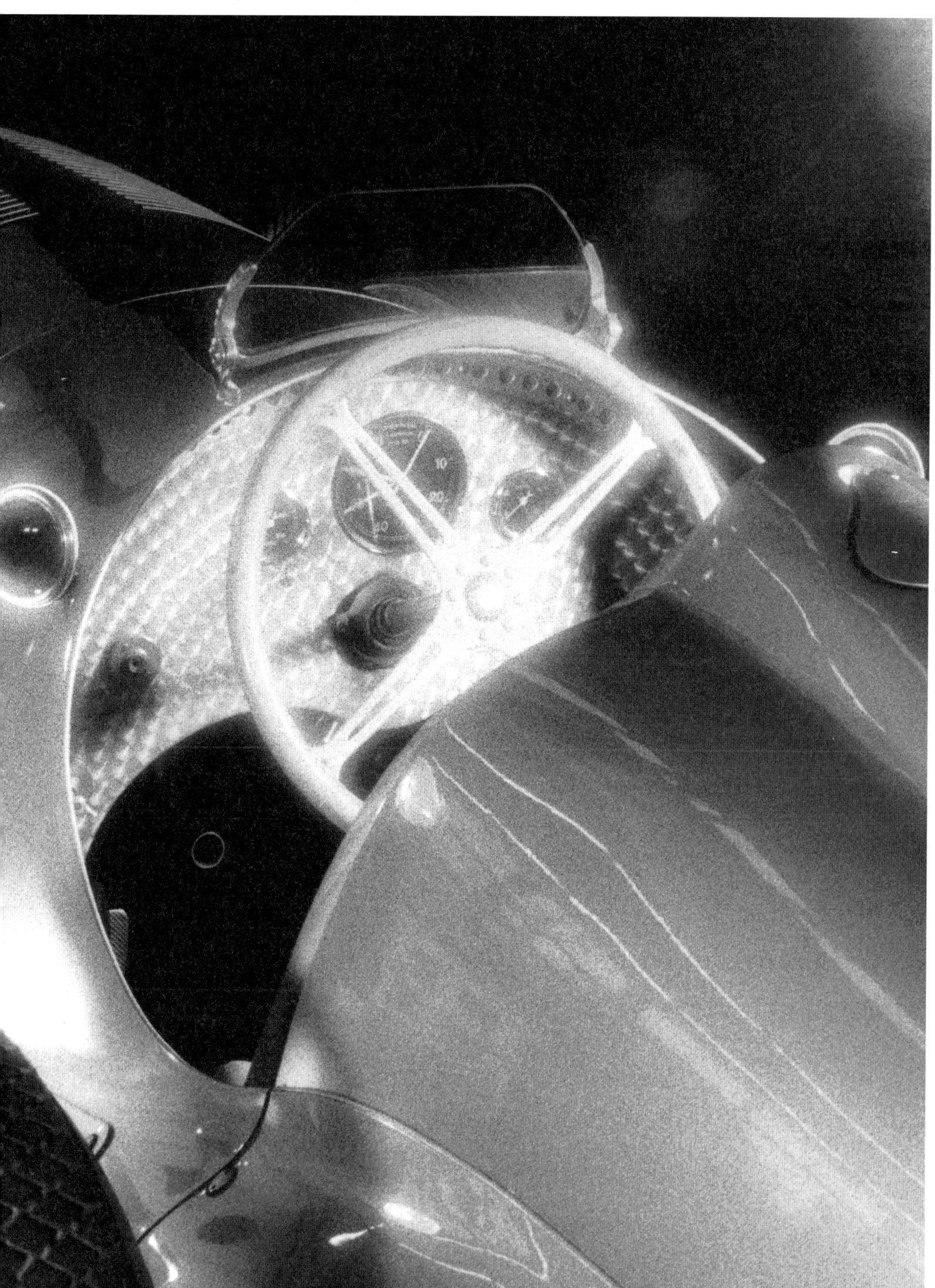

Shaped to fit the contours of its elongated form, the body of the Mercedes-Benz W125 was essentially dictated by the long, slender 8-cylinder in-line engine. The increased cooling air requirement of the more powerful W125 gave rise to one of its notable identifying characteristics – the triptych-like radiator grille

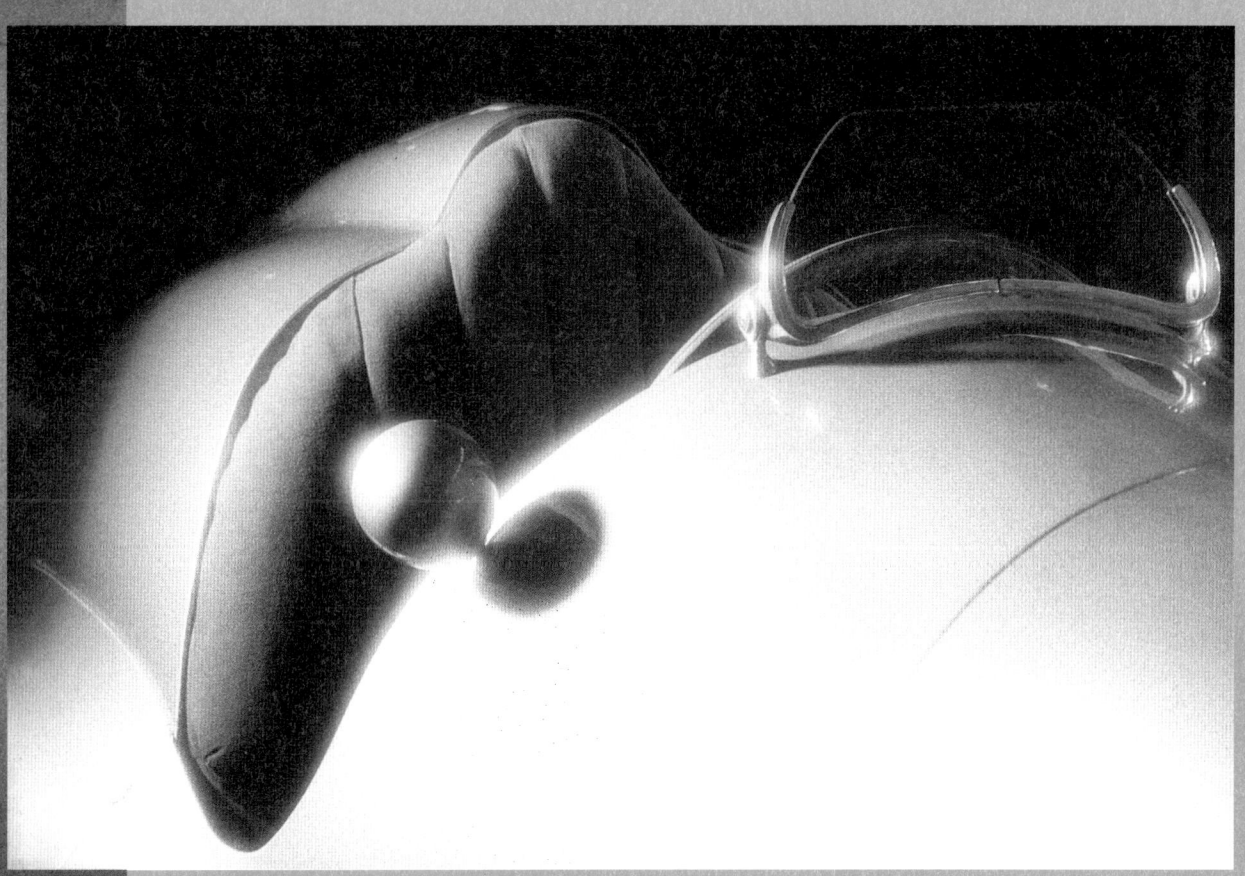

The cramped confines of the cockpit did not make the driver's job any easier: Grand Prix races went the full 500 kilometers and racing circuits were usually enough to make bone-shakers out of even the silkiest of machines

The Origin of the Silver Arrows

If everything had gone according to plan, nobody today would ever have heard of the term "Silver Arrows". "Whitefish", perhaps, though this was hardly a name to inspire generations of adoring enthusiasts. But things do not always turn out the way they were planned, calculated and constructed – even at Daimler-Benz, where perfection is the absolute yardstick in all things. And so it was in 1934, when a spontaneous solution was urgently sought to a 1000-gram problem.

For the Eifel race, which was to take place on June 3 that year, Mercedes-Benz had entered two works cars – both brand new and gleaming white. More powerful than most of the other Grand Prix cars parked in the drivers enclosure at the Nürburgring, this pair were without doubt race favorites, since the cars' designer Dr. Hans Nibel had tailored them with optimum precision to meet the specifications of the new formula for this most prestigious class of racing car. In truth, the new regulations prescribed little more than a maximum weight limit – excluding fuel, oils, coolant and tires – of 750 kg.

At the official weigh-in on the Saturday evening before the race, all other competitors were within the imposed limit. Only the two Mercedes of Manfred von Brauchitsch and Luigi Fagioli went over – tipping the scales at 751 kg. Minor adjustments carried out in the heat of practice had added weight to the cars. But technical inspectors were never ones to show leniency in such weighty matters. There was nothing else for it – the extra pounds had to be shed.

It was Alfred Neubauer, once a Mercedes driver himself and since 1926 the team manager, who faced the problem. He, of all people, knew how difficult it would be to find a quick and effective solution. The quite spontaneous ingenuity with which the nut was cracked, however, has since become the stuff of legend and is authentically documented by Neubauer in his autobiography

Männer, Frauen und Motoren

"You'd better think of something quick," said von Brauchitsch, "or else we'll definitely not be painting the town red tonight."

"Paint?" I thought. And at that very moment I had an idea. "Of course – the paintwork, that's the answer."

The mechanics worked through the night to rub down and scrape away every square inch of white paint, until by Sunday morning two mat-silver cars stood on the scales, weighing-in – according to Neubauer – at precisely 750 kg. Nowadays, of course, no racing team manager would even contemplate such an idea. To scratch off that highly lucrative sponsors' advertising would bring instant ruin to any team.

Driving the Mercedes W25, Manfred von Brauchitsch won the first ever race to feature the Silver Arrows. It was June 3, 1934. In second place, at the wheel of the new Auto Union car, was his compatriot and rival Hans Stuck. At this stage the Auto Union cars were still all in white, but it was not long before

Montlhery near Paris, the Mercedes W25 cars line up beside the pits in sled-dog formation. Rudolf Caracciola (above) fits snugly into the cramped cockpit

CARACCIOLA BECOMES
THREE TIMES EUROPEAN CHAMPION

silver was adopted by both teams as the new racing color for German cars – though with silver paint covering the bare aluminum, of course.

Although the legendary Silver Arrows can trace their appearance to the frantic paint-scraping on the eve of the race, the name itself was not coined until it appeared in print in a newspaper some years later. But as befits any truly great legend, the exact source remains clouded in mystery.

The fascination this early generation of Silver Arrows held for the masses was due in no small part to the charisma of their drivers. In those days, these sportsmen led the high-profile lifestyles of film stars. Caracciola and Co. would never arrive at the circuit for practice in anonymous leased cars, as their younger colleagues do today. Their arrival was always carefully staged in a red Mercedes convertible – lid down, of course – dressed not in anything so ordinary as a polo shirt and jeans, but posing in full racing whites. And all that just to get to the pits.

These were "gentleman racers" through and through, a breed apart who enjoyed the good life and preferred to drink champagne rather than shower in it on the victory rostrum. They ran up huge bills in expensive restaurants. In short, they led the sort of lives their enthusiastic fans could only dream of.

Within this realm of myths and legends it was rumored that there existed among the driving fraternity a kind of feudalistic social order which served to enforce subtle differences of class away from the race circuit. One anecdote, possibly apocryphal, which serves to illustrate the point, has it that Rudolf Caracciola once placed the following order at the bar: "Champagne for Herr von Brauchitsch and myself and a beer for our young colleague here, Hermann Lang."

These racing masters of yesteryear made no attempt to impress with displays of fitness and training programs, even if such things existed. In the hearts and minds of the public they were true heroes, because they endured races of 500 kilometers or more and faced extreme dangers. The frequent accidents – many of them fatal – lent the sport an element of high drama no longer acceptable in modern racing.

From 1934 onwards, the engineering and styling of the cars themselves began to add a new dimension to an already substantial public fascination for the sport. The 750-kg formula failed, however, in its primary objective – that of curbing speed around the circuits. In the years to come, the Silver Arrows were not alone in constantly bettering the power and speed of racing cars from earlier generations.

The new formula presented designers with a challenge in as far as it forced a return to the drawing board and offered the opportunity to work with fresh and revolutionary ideas to create a completely new generation of racing car. At Daimler-Benz such con-

Manfred von Brauchitsch wins the Eifel race in 1934. The blurring of early racing photos was due to the vertical shutter mechanism in cameras

Intense heat in the cockpit made driving thirsty work. Manfred von Brauchitsch takes a refreshing glass of cold water

cepts had existed a number of years earlier. Even before the roaring twenties had drawn to a close, it had become clear that the sporting days of the heavyweight two-ton SSK were numbered.

In order to compete against the lighter cars of constructors such as Alfa Romeo, Bugatti and Maserati, the Daimler-Benz technical department – where Ferdinand Porsche was still technical director – drew up plans for a racing car with a mid-engine. Two possible drive systems were considered – an 8-cylinder in-line and a 16-cylinder unit. The designer Otto Schilling had been working on just such a project: it was a 5-liter engine developing almost 350 hp. From 1933 onwards, Ferdinand Porsche – by this time working freelance for Auto Union – took these plans to further stages of development at his design offices in Stuttgart's Kronenstraße, just a stone's throw from the Daimler-Benz Untertürkheim site. Daimler-Benz, however, preferred to continue with

"tried-and-tested formulae"

and in 1934 introduced the highly conventional Mercedes W25 (W from the German for "car", Wagen). Designer of the running gear, Max Wagner, placed the engine in the usual position between driver and front axle. Only the drive concept differed slightly from standard practice: the differential and transmission positioned below it formed one distinct unit at the rear axle. This solution allowed for a low cardan shaft, low driver position and a more advantageous distribution of weight. The early trans-axle concept was feasible because the W25 – according to the fashion of the day – had a full-floating axle. With independent suspension and double wishbones at the front, it also boasted a swing axle rear end instead of the usual rigid axle.

Engine design experts Albert Heeß and Otto Schilling were entering the "arms race" of the dawning era with what one might call a rather conservative power train. Design of the engine bearing the type designation M 25 (M from the German for "engine", Motor) retained many of the proven and durable Mercedes concepts. It was clear that desire for success did not mean taking unnecessary risks. But dividends recouped from the work invested were reassuringly positive: the 8-cylinder engine with 3360 cm^3 developed 325 hp straight off. This design for an 8-cylinder in-line engine with twin overhead camshafts and four valves per cylinder went straight from the drawing board into the Mercedes-Benz history books. A racing engine of this design had been built as early as 1924 under the designation M 218 – commissioned by Ferdinand Porsche, though largely the work of the young engineer Wunibald Kamm. Thanks largely to his efforts, the 2-liter supercharged engine with a boost pressure of 0.98 bar generated 170 hp at 7000 rpm.

Design of the M 25 engine followed the old pattern, and in so doing exhibited a number of features which appear both astonishing and rather unexpected from the modern perspective. The crankcase of the old racing engine was made of light metal alloy and the eight cylinders of cast steel were held in place using tensile stays. The combustion chambers and the actual cylinder-head made up another steel element, which, like the metal casing of the water jackets surrounding the eight cylinders, was welded to the cylinder liners.

Bolted to this steel construction were the two camshaft casings of light metal alloy. Inside these, and driven by a vertical shaft drive, were the intake and exhaust camshafts.

Each of these activated the sixteen valves via two forked rocker arms. The Roots blower, mounted verti-

In Monaco the heavens serve refreshments to the victor Caracciola. But otherwise the so-called "Kurzer Wagen" (lit. short car), with its slightly modified appearance, does not bring the success hoped for

The 1930s | 27

cally in front of the engine, was driven continuously at twice the crankshaft speed, delivering air compressed to almost 1 bar via twin carburetors to the inlet valves.

A major difference between these Mercedes racing engines and modern engine design was in the crankshaft bearings. Whereas nowadays friction bearings enable everything from 6000 rpm in large-scale manufacturing to 18500 rpm in Formula One, the race engine designers chose the tried-and-tested anti-friction bearings favored in motorbike construction.

The arguments in favor of these preferred roller bearings were plentiful enough. For one thing, the bearing shells could not withstand high loads and, in addition, this close relation of the popular ball bearing posed fewer problems where oil was concerned.

They were not in need of a constant oil pressure, for example, in order to operate with minimal friction and without causing wear. Even when the oil supply was momentarily suspended during cornering, the shaft did not seize immediately. The amount of oil used by these old racing engines was no more than that required by small car crank assemblies today. In its first season the M 25A increased its output considerably. The 325 hp normally achieved under race conditions using the customary benzene/benzol mixture rose to 354 hp when the tank was filled with a heady mix of 86 % methylalcohol, 4.4 % nitrobenzene, 8.8 % acetone and 0.8 % ether. Clearly a concoction to be kept well out of the reach of children and domestic animals!

Sixty-seven years later a series production 6-cylinder Mercedes-Benz with approximately the same 3.2 liter displacement also achieves a respectable 354 hp using the same booster as its older relative: a mechanically driven supercharger. The difference, of course, is that the 2001 model relies on a rather less toxic fuel mix for its tank.

The output figures published by Auto Union in 1934 and also much later were, by comparison, extra-

In the face of stiff competition from the Mercedes-Benz Silver Arrows and Auto Union, Achille Varzi's Alfa Romeo and Tazio Nuvolari's Maserati were not able to get a look-in even on home soil in the 1934 Italian Grand Prix at Monza

The Monaco Grand Prix affords "gentleman driver" Rudolf Caracciola the perfect photo opportunity

ordinarily cautious. Their 16-cylinder 4356 cm³ engine officially recorded 295 hp in its first season.

Mercedes-Benz started 1934 with drivers Manfred von Brauchitsch, Luigi Fagioli and Rudolf Caracciola, who was still recovering from the results of an accident in Monaco the previous year and did not race until the German Grand Prix.

In 1934 the teams from Mercedes-Benz and Auto Union were very evenly matched – a fact amply demonstrated by the two races at the Nürburgring. Von Brauchitsch's Mercedes took victory in the Silver Arrows premiere at the Eifel race ahead of Hans Stuck driving for Auto Union, but the pendulum swung the other way in July at the German Grand Prix held on the same circuit. This time Hans Stuck won ahead of the Mercedes driven by the Italian Luigi Fagioli.

It was not just the Silver Arrows who found winning form in 1934. That same year was the start of a winning streak for the football club Schalke 04. Between 1934 – the year the club won its first championship title – and 1942, the club went on to take a further five German titles. In Austria, 1934 was the year that saw the completion of the Großglockner Pass over the Alps; the road would later be used for hillclimbs.

"The goal was 500 hp"

for the 1934 season. Messrs Heeß and Schilling spent a good deal of time laboring over their engine in order to maintain its "balance of power". By increasing the displacement to 3716 cm³ the output of the M 25 AB was improved to 395 hp.

During the winter break a 4-liter machine was developed – the M 25 B with 3990 cm³ giving 430 hp. And throughout 1935 the engineers experimented with an ultra long-stroke version – the M 25 C – which generated 462 hp and nearly 600 Newton meters of torque from a displacement of 4307 cm³.

The Mercedes-Benz team dominated the European racing scene throughout 1935. Rudolf Caracciola was back on top of his form, winning seven races and posting three new lap records. These wins brought him the first of his three European titles – as prestigious at the time as a World Championship today. Early signs suggested, however, that Auto Union was in no mood to throw in the towel. In 1935 the experienced Tazio Nuvolari was joined by a new teammate – the youthful Bernd Rosemeyer. In the Eifel race that year, Rosemeyer put up a heroic struggle with Rudolf Caracciola, the Mercedes driver only securing victory a few hundred yards from the finish. Later that fall, Rosemeyer won his first Grand Prix at Brno.

In 1936 the German Reich took its first tentative steps into the media age. The first official television broadcasting post was established in Berlin. Others were soon to follow, for the Ministry of Propaganda was determined to turn the 1936 Olympic Games into a media spectacle.

Alfred Neubauer, right, a trim figure in those days, has some good news: Tazio Nuvolari in the Bugatti is 15 seconds down. Tramlines running along the race circuit in San Sebastian were not then considered a problem

Britain was one step ahead, however. With the creation of the BBC, the nation had already put in place a public television service.

The Mercedes-Benz engineers believed they were well equipped to face the challenges of the 1936 season. The engine boys had squeezed every last drop of performance out of the 8-cylinder: with a bore and stroke of 86 millimeters and 102 millimeters respectively, its capacity of 4738 cm^3 was now capable of delivering 494 hp. Running gear expert Wagner had shortened the wheelbase from 2720 mm to 2460 mm. The cardan shaft was now positioned even lower, since comprehensive modifications had been made to the transmission on the rear axle. The four-wheel independent suspension with swing axle to the rear had been replaced by a rigid De Dion layout in an effort to counteract the car's tendency to oversteer now that output was just a shade under 500 hp. An external sign of the modernization of the W25 – year of construction 1936 and dubbed "Kurzer Wagen" (lit. "short car") – was its more slender body shell.

Following the glittering success of the previous year, the 1936 season could scarcely have begun more promisingly: Caracciola took first place in Monte Carlo and Tunis and finished second in Barcelona. But things took a sudden turn at the Eifel race, where Rosemeyer came out the winner; a week later in Budapest it was Nuvolari who took the honors.

The Mercedes-Benz team was beginning to experience an increasing number of headaches with the new cars. Cracks in the front cylinders suggested that the extreme increase in power was too much for the

Alfred Neubauer, deep in strategic discussion, had already put on a few pounds by the time the Mercedes W125 was developed

Sporting gentlemen of the 1930s wore flat caps and were strong enough to load the 750-kg W125 using nothing but brawn and their bare hands

engine. And difficulties with directional stability aroused suspicions that the wheelbase was now a fraction too short. When all Mercedes cars failed to finish at Budapest, Alfred Neubauer imposed a cessation of racing activities. The team dropped out of two races. At this point, fundamental changes were made to the way in which motor sport development was organized. Racing engineering would henceforth no longer simply be a spin-off of series production development – Neubauer instigated an autonomous racing department and made Rudolf Uhlenhaut its director.

Before long this appointment would prove to be a stroke of genius, although the talents of this 30-year-old engineer were initially by no means fully apparent. Uhlenhaut had been with Daimler-Benz AG for five years, where as a research engineer he had been in charge of the successful Mercedes 170 V. In addition, he had also notched up a number of successes in motor sport, having twice competed in the 2000-kilometer race. In 1933, driving a Mercedes 200, he shared victory in the team title, and in 1934, with the much more powerful and elegantly engineered Mercedes 500 K, he brought back individual gold.

In an attempt to get to the bottom of the problematic handling characteristics besetting their racing cars, Mercedes-Benz carried out extensive testing at the Nürburgring in August 1936. The importance attached to these tests is underlined by the fact that technical director Max Sailer and the new head of passenger car design Hans Gustav Röhr were also present at the "Ring". The drivers were Manfred von Brauchitsch and Rudolf Caracciola; four cars were at their disposal – two long wheelbase versions from 1935 and two of the 1936 short versions.

Rudolf Uhlenhaut carried out a highly systematic series of tests. Two days – and 25 tuning modifications – later Caracciola declared the problem solved and the cars to be in race condition. So he and von Brauchitsch set off with two of the cars to compete in the Swiss Grand Prix in Bern.

But the research team left behind at the Nürburgring continued its work with the remaining two cars. The test driver was now Rudolf Uhlenhaut, who until this point had never before taken the wheel of a Grand Prix car, but by all accounts made a pretty good job of his first attempt. After further testing he suggested a number of other improvements.

Most importantly of all, however, he established that a number of fundamental modifications were necessary. The front axle needed longer wishbones in order to reduce the effect of camber changes on the wheels and to maintain correct steering geometry during spring compression. His tests also revealed that circuits such as the one at the Nürburgring – and, indeed, the surfaces of a number of other Grand Prix tracks – were not best dealt with by meeting force with force. This was to be the principle of

"Uhlenhaut's revolution"

As the engineer explained: "In future we shall need to look for ways of achieving substantially greater spring travel." Clearly his own experience on the Nürburgring presented him with the key to a revolutionary tuning concept of soft springs and hard dampers – an approach which flew in the face of all received wisdom for the circuit.

Proof – if proof be needed – of the quality of Czech carpentry: a grandstand view at the Masaryk Ring in Brno for a group of early freeclimbers

In Monte Carlo, viewing points for spectators have an altogether different charm. Manfred von Brauchitsch and Rudolf Caracciola battle for victory in 1937

At the Swiss Grand Prix the drivers may have declared themselves happy with the handling characteristics of their cars, but less so, perhaps, with the outcome of the race. Not only were Caracciola and von Brauchitsch forced to retire, but Fagioli also failed finish. Engine failure was the obvious cause in two of the cases, but Caracciola's car revealed a dangerous weakness in the running gear: the tubular cross-member of the De Dion axle had come away on the right-hand side. For this reason Alfred Neubauer decided to abandon the last important race of the 1936 season, the Italian Grand Prix.

The Auto Union team came out clear winners in the 1936 races, the young Bernd Rosemeyer finishing his second season with the works team with a total of seven wins, three of them Grand Prix victories. He took the European title and also became German hill-climb and road race champion.

The Olympic Games held in Berlin were the major event of the summer of 1936. As planned, the events were indeed broadcast using a small network of television cameras. Most of the German nation, however, followed the fortunes of its sporting heroes on the radio – even though germanicizing of the language meant they were no longer officially permitted to refer to such a device as "ein Radio".

Work in the race department at Daimler-Benz AG during the autumn of 1936 focused on the development of a completely new car – the W125. Max Wagner began with the chassis. Here he was able to introduce into motor sport some of the insights gained from series production. As with the Mercedes 170 V, for example, he employed two generously dimen-

The 1938 Coppa Acerbo in Pescara in Italy's deep south. On the front line of the grid is Tazio Nuvolari (Auto Union) alongside Mercedes drivers Manfred von Brauchitsch and Hermann Lang

Nürburgring 1938: a complete tire change still takes 42 seconds, since only three mechanics are allowed to work on the car during pit stops. The uniformed gentleman from the local NSKK keeps a watchful eye on proceedings

sioned oval-section steel tubes as longitudinal members for the frame. This traditional ladder structure, with its four cross-members, is now generally found only in classic off-road vehicles and pick-ups.

Attempts to lengthen spring travel led to the development of a new front axle. The double wishbones had become significantly longer, though at 250 mm for the upper and 300 mm for the lower they were not even half the length they are today. The distance of spring travel achieved was many times in excess of what is commonly required for smooth modern circuits. On compression, 75 mm of positive travel were available, and on rebound there was a maximum negative travel of 70 mm.

Instead of the out-dated quarter-elliptic leaf springs, the De Dion rear axle was given correct guidance with longitudinal control arms and torsion bars – like its Zwickau-based competitors. Rear spring travel was even more spectacular than at the front: 90 mm positive and 90 mm negative. Now the correct, taut cushioning could be supplied by hydraulic lever-type shock absorbers working alongside old-fashioned friction-plate shock absorbers.

The M 25 E engine had reached the limits of its possibilities, and the intractable problems it was throwing up now called for a radical solution. The plan to replace the 8-cylinder in-line unit with a V 12 had been abandoned six months earlier. The mighty 5577 cm³ machine had excelled on the test rig with 575 hp, but failed at the weigh-in, tipping the scales at a fighting weight of 300 kg. It was now time for

"a show of force with 646 hp."

In 1936 developments got underway for a lengthened version of the 8-cylinder engine – Type M 125 – in which the spacing of the cylinders was increased from 95 to 104 mm. In this way a significant amount of room was created for larger cylinders – 94 mm x 102 mm gave a new displacement of 5660 cm³, surpassing even the 12-cylinder unit. The engine

The British driver Richard Seaman drove his last race at the 1939 Belgian Grand Prix in Spa Francorchamps. Seen here gliding through "La Source" in pouring rain, he hit a tree shortly afterwards, sending his Mercedes-Benz up in flames

Anatomy of a lightweight

The very first Silver Arrow was limited to just 750 kilograms, excluding coolant, oil, fuel and tires. Race-ready, it weighed 847 kilograms. As a consequence, its overall dimensions were surprisingly modest – at just 4040 millimeters it was barely longer than today's Mercedes SLK.

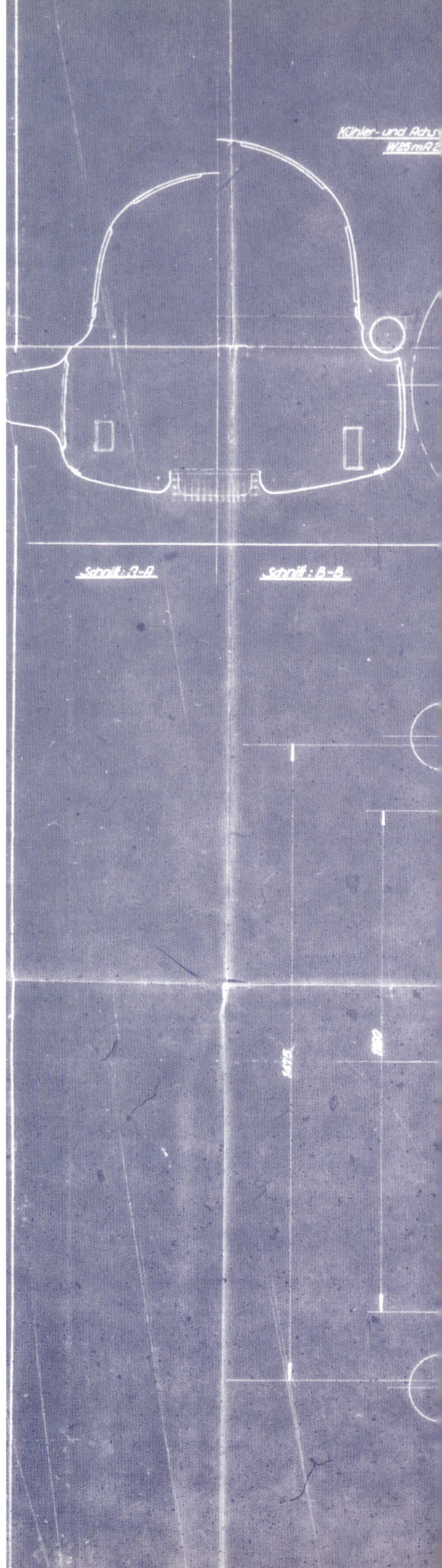

At the 1938 German Grand Prix the circuit leaves much to be desired, but the race order will have given Don Alfredo Neubauer something to smile about

traffic tailbacks before and after the race, but the more youthful fans made the pilgrimage to the hilly Eifel region on bicycle or took one of the special trains laid on by the Reichsbahn to the nearby town of Adenau. And for the many obliged to stay at home, the radio – by this time a standard feature of almost every household – transmitted the race commentary over the airwaves.

The end of the 1937 season was also the end of the monster engines, however. From 1938 a new formula was to take effect: supercharged engines were permitted a maximum 3 liters, naturally aspirated engines only 4.5 liters.

Mercedes-Benz, Auto Union and Alfa Romeo remained faithful to the compressor, and the result of the new formula was to bring the two German teams appreciably closer in engineering terms. Both designed their 3-liter engines as a V12 unit arranged in two rows of six cylinders at 60 degrees. The Mercedes design was the more extravagant of the two, with its four overhead camshafts and four valves. Robert von Eberan-Eberhorst, the new race engine designer at Auto Union, contented himself with three overhead camshafts and two-valve technology.

The new M 154 engine was not unrelated to earlier 12-cylinder projects. Here, for example, the combustion chambers and the metal casing surrounding the water-jackets were once again welded onto the cylinders. But the engine, with no fewer than seven roller bearings, achieved its output more from engine speed. Whereas all 8-cylinder engines between 1934 and 1937 had the same rated speed of 5800 rpm, that figure had now gone up to a slick 8000 rpm.

The engine now used an alcohol mix as standard, and with a booster pressure of 1.3 bar it immediately achieved 427 hp at 8000 rpm. Before long, this had been bettered to 466 hp and even reached 474 hp later in the season. The quest for trouble-free improved performance, whilst at the same time avoiding heat overload, led Rudolf Uhlenhaut to carry out a number of tests using various compression ratios, boost pressures and valve control times.

Eventually the Mercedes 12-cylinder cars lined up for the race with a rating of 450 hp – moderate by 1938 standards, and modest, too, when compared with the 485 hp at 7000 rpm claimed by the Auto Union engines. But Mercedes came away with the better balance sheet: of the four GP races for the European Championship, three went to the cars with the three-pointed star, just one to Auto Union.

Celebration of these successes would be premature, however, as there remained an important issue to resolve. The high performance of these 3-liter engines, coupled with the low calorific content of the alcohol mix used to cool the cylinders so effectively, meant extremely high fuel consumption. And since refueling using milk churns was both a laborious and thoroughly dangerous business, it was conceivable that the less powerful, but more fuel-efficient, 4.5-liter naturally aspirated engines might offer unwanted competition.

Indeed this is exactly what René Dreyfus – driving a Delahaye in the 1938 French Grand Prix in Pau – succeeded in proving in front of the assembled "compressor club". He completed the entire race distance on one tank, leaving the thirsty Mercedes of Caracciola and Lang trailing in his wake.

At the 1938 Coppa Ciano in Livorno, Manfred von Brauchitsch discovers that Italy has the best-dressed policemen as well as drugstores selling wines, spirits and tobacco

Anatomy of a dwarf

The Mercedes W165 is the smallest of all Silver Arrows: at just 3680 millimeters it is a fraction longer than today's A-Class. Its engine, too, is smaller than any other Mercedes Grand Prix racing car. The V8 1498 cm³ engine develops 254 hp at 8000 rpm. At 195 kilograms, though, it is twice as heavy as the current V10 3-liter racing engine giving over 800 hp.

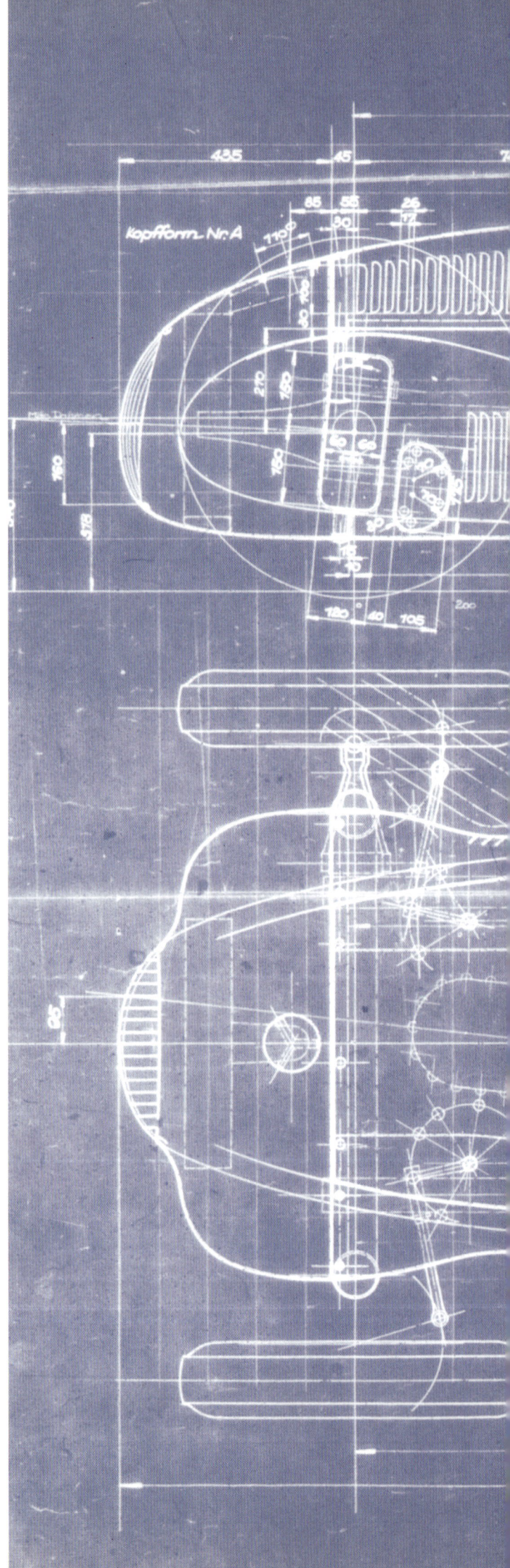

with a maximum displacement of 1.5 liters. Both Alfa Romeo and Maserati had "monoposto" designs which conformed to this requirement, but the all-conquering Germans with their Silver Arrows did not. That the

"challenge of Tripoli"

was taken up both by Mercedes-Benz and by Auto Union, seems unexpectedly far-sighted. Far from turning their attentions to the prospect of a World War, the teams' racing strategists were faced with an altogether different dilemma. The new formula reduced displacement in compressor engines to 1.5 liters, whilst normally aspirated engines were permitted 4.5 liters.

Eight months before the race, work got underway in Stuttgart to design and build the W165, which was to be fitted with a V8 engine. At the same time, the Zwickau engineers set about constructing a V12 engine for a racing car in this class. If the performance statistics were anything to go by, all seemed to be going very well in the "race to the starting line" for the team from Saxony. The Auto Union V12's 1481 cm^3 gave 327 hp at 8500 rpm, whereas the 1491 cm^3 Mercedes V8 engine developed a mere 275 hp at 8200 rpm. But the "race to the starting line" would only be won by the team that actually made it to the grid. And lined up at the start in Tripoli were two Mercedes – one driven by Hermann Lang, the race's eventual winner, and the other by the second-placed Rudolf Caracciola. Unable to get their cars ready in time, the Auto Union cars never made it to the final showdown before the outbreak of war.

Fittingly, "Gone with the Wind" won the Oscar in 1939 for best picture. Just a few months later, the first generation of Silver Arrows was also exactly that – "gone with the wind".

In the early years of racing, teams were bigger than they are today. Back in 1938 Mercedes-Benz set off for Tripoli with four racing cars

At the port in Naples, medieval methods are required to help load the cars onto a ship bound for Libya. A 2 hp transporter delivers the 575 hp Mercedes W125 to the quayside

Under Rudolf
Uhlenhaut's guidance,
Mercedes-Benz racing
cars reached technical
perfection and
acquired even
greater elegance

W154

Mercedes-Benz responded to the challenge set down by a new formula in 1938 with their W154. From now on supercharged engines were restricted to a 3-liter displacement, with a maximum 4.5 liters for normally aspirated engines. But before long, performance had begun to escalate as before. The Mercedes-Benz Silver Arrows started the season with a 12-cylinder engine which developed 450 hp

Driving the Mercedes W154, Rudolf Caracciola became European Champion for the third time in 1938 and Hermann Lang took his first title in 1939 – an achievement on a par with a World Championship today. Having learned their lessons from the so-called "Kurzer Wagen", the engineers ultimately opted for the longer wheelbase version of the W154

A glimpse into the cockpit from such a sublime vantagepoint reveals the comfortable handcrafted upholstery of the racing car interior. Seating in the Mercedes-Benz W154 was positively cozy for such long races compared with earlier models. The instrument panel still only featured the essentials, however. The adjustable windscreen was baptized "Brooklands"

The Mercedes-Benz W165 started in just one race, winning the 1939 Grand Prix in Tripoli. By the time the regulations for which the car was built finally came into force after the Second World War, the earlier champion from Tripoli had long since been overtaken

The W165 was the "Baby Benz" in the Silver Arrow family of the 1930s. It was designed and built in the record time of just eight months so that it could take its place at the start of the Tripoli Grand Prix in Libya on May 7, 1939. The smallest of its generation, the W165 had only a 1.5-liter displacement, yet developed 275 hp at 8200 rpm. It thus not only conformed to the new minimum regulations imposed for the race in North Africa, but also to proposals to introduce a new formula which would restrict supercharged engines to 1.5 liters and normally aspirated engines to 4.5 liters

Six decades ago the "gentlemen drivers" were still racing on astonishingly narrow tires with a relatively large diameter – 5 x 17 ins. at the front, and 6 x 17 ins. at the rear. In those days the narrow tires were supplied by Continental. Today the Mercedes W165 sports Dunlops

During wheel changes back in 1939 the quick-release wing nuts on the wheels were still loosened in the traditional way with a blow from a copper hammer. Traditional, too, were the wire-spoke wheels, which would accompany a second generation of Silver Arrows fifteen years later.

MANFRED VON

Drivers of the 1930s

Manfred von Brauchitsch's curriculum vitae not only documents a great career as a racing driver, it paints a remarkable portrait of that period of twentieth century German history into which he was fatefully born.

The young von Brauchitsch, born on August 15, 1905, grew up in Berlin in a Prussian military family. His father Victor von Brauchitsch was a major in the Royal Prussian army, and his uncle Walter was also about to embark on a glittering military career. He would later be appointed Field Marshall General in 1938, and from 1939 onwards was to command the German armed forces in the military campaigns against Poland, France, Yugoslavia and Greece. His commission came to an abrupt end, however, during the Russian campaign as a result of his differences with Adolf Hitler.

"The continuation"

of the story shows that defeat for Germany in the First World War did not oblige the von Brauchitsch family to break with tradition. For Manfred, too, life began in earnest with a military training – although becoming a soldier at that time was anything but easy. The Treaty of Versailles permitted Germany to keep only very limited armed forces – the Reichswehr, an army of one hundred thousand men. But the family had friends in high places, and in January 1923, having left grammar school at 17, the young Herr von Brauchitsch joined up as a sapper with a unit stationed in the Spandau citadel in Berlin.

Manfred von Brauchitsch later described this unit in his book "Kampf um Meter und Sekunden" as a pitiful bunch of soldiers in secondhand uniforms and worn-out boots. The sappers were only allowed to leave the citadel wearing civilian clothes, for reasons which became clear when, later that year, the tiny unit was disbanded. According to the letter of the Treaty of Versailles, these soldiers did not constitute a legal reinforcement of the Reichswehr.

Eventually young Manfred's family got him started on the right path, and on New Year's Day 1924 he took up a placement as an officer cadet in the company of the Fifth Infantry stationed in the garrison town of Stettin. During his time in the army, he successfully completed his school leaving certificate – a requirement for any aspiring officer – and passed both his ensign training and the entrance examination for the firearms school in Dresden.

"In the fall of 1928"

he completed his training in Dresden and Manfred von Brauchitsch was able to return to his unit in Stettin as a fully-fledged ensign. But his military career was to come to a sudden and unforeseen end.

Von Brauchitsch received an inheritance, and with this the junior officer was able to fulfil a dream. He bought a motorbike. Not just any motorbike, you understand, but a BMW.

Late one afternoon, having finished his duties for the day, Manfred von Brauchitsch hurriedly set off on the BMW in the direction of the airport to catch a flight from Stettin to visit his parents in Berlin. But the turnip harvest was underway and strewn across a bend in the road were discarded turnip leaves.

Back at the garrison's military hospital, the medical officer pronounced an extensive diagnosis – fracture to the base of the skull, broken collarbone, six broken ribs and paralysis to one side of the face. Three months later, the ensign Manfred von Brauchitsch was released from hospital but declared unfit to continue serving in the Reichswehr.

The family decided he needed to spend some time recuperating in the

BRAUCHITSCH

A group photograph of the Mercedes team in 1938: Manfred von Brauchitsch, Alfred Neubauer, Dick Seaman, Hermann Lang and Rudi Caracciola

Herr von Brauchitsch did not just restrict himself to mineral water to quench his thirst – champagne would do just as well

country. So at the invitation of his cousin Hans Ulrich von Zimmermann he was sent to the royal estate at Nischwitz near Leipzig.

Manfred von Brauchitsch soon discovered in his cousin a kindred spirit and an irrepressible motor enthusiast. The extensive garage attached to the imposing estate in 1928 housed no fewer than three automobiles, of which one was a supercharged Mercedes.

To begin with Manfred was content to enjoy the car's power from the passenger seat. But before long – with his enthusiasm for motorbikes beginning to wane – he began driving the vehicle around the estate by himself. There was still the small matter of a driving license, however. Manfred von Brauchitsch described himself as "a driving instructor's worst nightmare," and evidently the final lesson before his test brought relief to teacher and pupil in equal measures. But at last Manfred could take the Mercedes for a spin without breaking the law.

His decision to become a racing driver crystallized when he caught a glimpse of his first motor race on the weekly news broadcast at the cinema. And from the very outset, von Brauchitsch demonstrated a remarkably professional attitude to the job. He declared that anyone hoping to become a top driver must first understand the workings of the car.

He went immediately to train as a mechanic at Hermann Bieler's workshop, his six-month apprenticeship lasting until the spring of 1929. Having become a close friend of Bieler, Manfred von Brauchitsch then decided he was equipped well enough to quit the workshop.

That same year the two cousins, Hans Ulrich and Manfred, moved to Berchtesgaden in Bavaria in pursuit of a career in motor sport. To get this underway, von Brauchitsch resorted to the rather peculiar practice of the period. He took the supercharged Mercedes to Leipzig, where he had the local automobile club confirm in writing his starting time. He then drove as fast as he could to the automobile club in Berchtesgaden to have his arrival time rubber-stamped. This document then served as a valid record of sporting achievement.

The races organized towards the end of the 1920s were also often of a

The 1930s | 61

Alfred Neubauer and Manfred von Brauchitsch enjoyed a close friendship for many years. This came to an end when the driver became an instrument of socialist politics in the GDR

rather peculiar nature. Manfred von Brauchitsch tells, for example, of a "12-hour non-stop cross-country race" across the whole of Bavaria – the winner being the driver to cover the greatest distance.

Such a bold display of ambition persuaded uncle Hans von Zimmermann to come up with a generous offer of sponsorship for his nephew. Digging deep into his pockets, he came up with 35,000 Reichsmarks for a Mercedes SS, whose 7-liter 6-cylinder supercharged engine developed an impressive 225 hp.

"In the fall of 1929"

the ambitious young von Brauchitsch was busy preparing for his first race on the Gaisberg in the nearby Salzkammergut mountains. Principally, this entailed secret training on the 12 kilometers of graveled road at the wheel of his supercharged Mercedes.

After three further days of official practice, Manfred von Brauchitsch was beginning to get the hang of the Gaisberg course. Star competitors such as Rudolf Caracciola or Hans Stuck were still recording slightly better times. But then they were driving two-seater sports cars, whereas he had entered the four-seater touring car category for engines of 3000 cm^3 and above, and in place of passengers he was obliged to carry sandbags weighing 65 kg. He won the category.

For the 1930 season, von Brauchitsch exchanged the four-seater SS for the shorter two-seater SSK. The following year, 1931, the SSK then shed a further 120 kg to become the SSKL, similar to the works racing car driven by Rudolf Caracciola.

But Manfred von Brauchitsch's funds at the time permitted only a handful of races per year, his successes coming predominantly in hill-climbs. With this in mind, the young von Brauchitsch decided in 1932 to undertake an ambitious project.

Aerodynamics specialist Baron Reinhard von Koenig-Fachsenfeld had designed a specially streamlined racing car for high-speed racing on the Avus. The body shell of this zeppelin on wheels was built by the Cannstatt firm of coachbuilders Vetter and was offered to Manfred von Brauchitsch at a bargain price of 500 Reichsmarks. The deal was struck: von Brauchitsch had the body fitted and set off immediately for Berlin with his unique machine.

"Problems"

with the as yet untested design only came to light during practice on the Avus circuit, where he found it impossible to overcome the difficulties caused by overheating. So despite having a superior car – with its 270 hp the streamlined Mercedes could top 230 km/h on the straights – Manfred von Brauchitsch was forced to drive a tactical race.

As, one by one, the competition was forced to retire, the race came down to a duel between von Brauchitsch and Rudolf Caracciola. Caracciola's Alfa Romeo was finally beaten on the finishing straight, where the Mercedes SSKL showed a defiantly superior turn of speed. Its average of 194.2 km/h for the race was not only a record for the Avus, but also set a new world best distance for the one hour mark.

"Overnight"

the handsome young nobleman became the object of public attention. Majestic Film GmbH saw him as an obvious choice to play the male lead in their forthcoming film "Kampf", and in his memoirs Manfred von Brauchitsch gives one good reason for accepting the role. "The 500 Marks for the streamlined body still had to be paid for."

Once filming was over, the young star bade farewell to that particular branch of show business, for his heart still lay in motor racing. His commitment was rewarded in 1934 with a works contract countersigned by Alfred Neubauer.

Victory at the Silver Arrows premiere on the Nürburgring in the 1934 Eifel race served to establish von Brauchitsch's place in the Mercedes team. He stayed until 1939, but his roles throughout this period were as often as not tragic ones. Ironically, the Nürburgring was also the circuit which brought his first season to a premature end. A serious crash during the German Grand Prix in July 1934 led to another lengthy period of convalescence at a sanatorium. Four years later, and once again at the Grand Prix raced at the foot of the Nürburg mountain, his Mercedes caught fire during refueling in the pits. Alfred Neubauer dragged von Brauchitsch from the cockpit with his own hands. Miraculously the driver escaped uninjured. But with the flames quickly extinguished and before the pit stop team knew what was happening, a pumped-up von Brauchitsch climbed back in and set off again. On reaching the airfield – one of the fastest sections of the Nordschleife – he discovered that the steering wheel had not been locked into position. It came away in his hands and von Brauchitsch had to steer a course by turning the toothed cogs at the end of the steering column. Somehow he managed to come to a standstill without causing further harm to himself or the car.

Manfred von Brauchitsch rounded off his personal record of successes with two Grand Prix victories in 1939. But all attempts to return to winning ways after the Second World War failed. In his disappointment and desperation – the causes of which were many and ran deep – he took up residence in the other Germany in the East.

In the GDR Manfred von Brauchitsch carved out a career in politics. In 1957 he became Sports President of the East German Motor Sport Association (AdMV) and in 1960 he was elected President of the Olympic Society of the GDR. Today Manfred von Brauchitsch lives with his wife Lotti in Thuringia.

Rudolf Caracciola's face reveals what it was really like to drive a 500-kilometer race six decades ago. His make-up invites the reader to draw one or two conclusions about the engine's oil consumption

Nobody dominated racing during the first generation of Mercedes Silver Arrows more than Rudolf Caracciola.

The name Caracciola is known not merely to devotees of motor sport — it has passed into the realm of general knowledge. For there are only a handful of drivers to have notched up over one hundred race victories in a lifetime.

The career of Otto Wilhelm Rudolf Caracciola reaches right back to the beginning of the last century.

The boy with the Italian surname was born in the town of Remagen in the German Rhineland on January 30, 1901 – the fourth child of Maximilian and Mathilde Caracciola.

But the Italian roots of the Caracciola family had been pulled up long ago. During the Thirty Years War, a certain Prince Bartolomeo Caracciolo commanded the fortress at Ehrenbreitstein near Coblenz. Evidently the Prince from Naples found the German Rhineland an agreeable area to live. He founded a family there, which over the centuries settled throughout the region and finally opted for the spelling Caracciola.

"The Remagen"

Caracciolas lived in relative prosperity in those early days. They owned the well-known and popular Hotel Caracciola. A passage in Caracciola's autobiography describes the young Rudi as something of a tearaway, who was forever "borrowing" the family Mercedes for illegal jaunts.

His boyhood dream of becoming a racing driver did not distract him from his studies, however. As well as gaining a driving license by the age of eighteen, he also completed his school leaving certificate just after the end of the First World War.

His father had died in 1915, but the young Caracciola showed no desire to take over the family hotel. As a small boy he had always been intrigued to discover how things worked, so he decided to start out in life as a trainee with a firm of mechanical engineers in Cologne. He subsequently moved to Aachen to work for an automobile manufacturer by the name of Fafnir, specializing in small, sporty models.

"During this period"

he achieved his first successes in motor sport – on two wheels – racing his NSU in endurance events. When Fafnir decided in 1922 to take part in the inaugural race at the Avus in Berlin, Rudi used the fine art of persuasion to get himself behind the wheel of one of the works cars. He finished the race fourth in his class and first among the Fafnir drivers.

Following a brawl with a Belgian soldier from the occupying forces in the Kakadu Bar in Aachen in 1923 – that area of Germany had been under occupation since the end of the First World War – Caracciola was forced to leave the Rhine and head for Dresden. There he set himself up as a car dealer, at first working for Fafnir. But before long he was offered a contract as a "sales official" from the Daimler-Motoren-Gesellschaft. Rudi spent his weekends racing a 1.5-liter Compressor for Daimler, and after eight races and four victories, it was not difficult to see where the main focus of his interest lay. With his dream of becoming a racing driver all but fulfilled, he finally abandoned his plans to study mechanical engineering.

"His statistics"

for the year 1924 were already beginning to read like those of a professional driver. Caracciola had fifteen wins in a Mercedes, including a notable victory at the renowned Klausenpass hill-climb in Switzerland.

In 1925 Rudolf Caracciola again began the season driving the small 4-cylinder compressor and by the end had notched up five more victories. 1926 was the year of the great breakthrough. Despite the wet conditions, Caracciola's victory with the 2-liter 8-cylinder compressor in front of 230,000 spectators at the Avus circuit returned an average speed of 135.1 km/h. The new racing car, with its 170 hp engine, was the work of Ferdinand Porsche, at that time technical director at Daimler.

Rudolf Caracciola shrewdly invested his prize money from the Avus race in a Mercedes dealership with cachet – prestigiously positioned on the Kurfürstendamm in Berlin.

Director Porsche also rendered outstanding services to Mercedes, designing a model series of larger sports cars, whose mighty 6-cylinder compressor engines began life with a 6.3 liter displacement giving a maximum output of 140 hp, and in the course of their development increased their capacity to seven liters with a peak output of 300 hp.

Before long, the Mercedes family was joined by a number of new additions – the so-called "White Elephants" – the Mercedes SS, SSK and SSKL. The astonishing potential of these cars was proved by Caracciola as early as 1926 with a victory at the Semmering hill-climb in Austria. And respect for both driver and car increased when, at the inaugural race at the new Nürburgring in 1927, Caracciola drove his Mercedes SSKL to victory and also set a new hill-climb record on the Klausenpass. In 1928 at the Sports Car Grand Prix, Caracciola again won at the Nürburgring, this time with mechanic Christian Werner as co-pilot. In addition, he recorded the fastest time on the hill-climb at Schauinsland near Freiburg, as well as on four other hill-climbs.

Caracciola did not specialize in any one particular motoring discipline, as is the practice today; his field was simply motor sport. He regularly represented Mercedes at the automobile tournament in Baden-Baden, and in 1929 he won the Austrian Alpine race and the 1930 Monte Carlo Rally.

This was also the year in which he first accepted the Mille Miglia challenge in Italy, scoring a class victory on his debut with Werner. In

A victorious Caracciola is stormed by the media. He was clearly also a firm favorite with the ladies

1931, however, he became the first foreign driver to win the Mille Miglia, this time driving the Mercedes SSKL with support from his mechanic Sebastian. He also notched up other wins at the Eifel race, the German Grand Prix, the Avus race and seven hill-climbs.

In the 1932 season, when Mercedes-Benz had a break from the motor racing scene for a while, Rudolf Caracciola drove for Alfa Romeo. He won the German Grand Prix on the Nürburgring, but was beaten into second place on the Avus circuit by the Mercedes SSKL of Manfred von Brauchitsch.

When Alfa Romeo withdrew from motor racing in 1933, Rudolf Caracciola and Louis Chiron founded the Scuderia CC. They bought two racing cars from Alfa, Mercedes-Benz supplying the race transporter.

The Monaco Grand Prix was the first race for Scuderia – and the last of the season for Caracciola. He skidded when one of his brakes locked, crashing into a flight of stone steps. He was taken to the Monte Carlo hospital with a shattered right thighbone and spent the next seven months convalescing in a specialist clinic in Bologna. With time, the fracture healed, but his right leg was now five centimeters shorter than his left. Caracciola left the clinic still wearing a plaster cast and in considerable pain.

In February 1934 fate delivered a second stroke of ill fortune. Charlotte, Carracciola's wife and known to all as Charly, was lost in an avalanche on a skiing trip.

Although Caracciola had every reason to be depressed, he remained optimistic. For 1934 was to be the start of a new chapter in motor racing, and he knew that with Mercedes-Benz once again in the running, this was where his next great opportunity lay.

"On April 2, 1934"

Caracciola drove a lap of honor before the start of the Monaco Grand Prix. On April 24 he took part in testing for Mercedes on the Avus circuit. And on July 15 Rudolf Caracciola lined up for the start of the German Grand Prix at the Nürburgring. Engine failure caused him to retire from that race, but later the same year he and Fagioli co-drove the winning car to take the Italian Grand Prix in Monza. Furthermore, during the hill-climb on the Klausenpass he established a record time that would never be broken.

The greatest period for Rudolf Caracciola with the Silver Arrows began in 1935, when he became European Champion for the first time. And he was to collect the title on two further occasions, in 1937 and 1938. In the five years leading up to the outbreak of the Second World War in 1939, he won no fewer than 16 Grand Prix titles.

Caracciola's comeback after the Second World War was short-lived. In his first season with Mercedes in 1952 a locked wheel – this time at the Swiss Grand Prix – was once again his undoing. His Mercedes 300 SL skidded into a tree, resulting in a serious fracture of his left leg.

With that, Rudolf Caracciola bade farewell to motor racing and retired to his Casa Scania in Lugano. He died on September 28th, 1959.

In Caracciola's day even the great racing drivers traveled to work by car – wherever that happened to be. En route for Pescara, Hermann Lang, Manfred von Brauchitsch and the folk hero known to his adoring fans simply as "Caratch" take a break in the shade of the trees

The sensual, flowing lines of the streamlined body build closely on the incomparable elegance of the Mercedes 300 SL

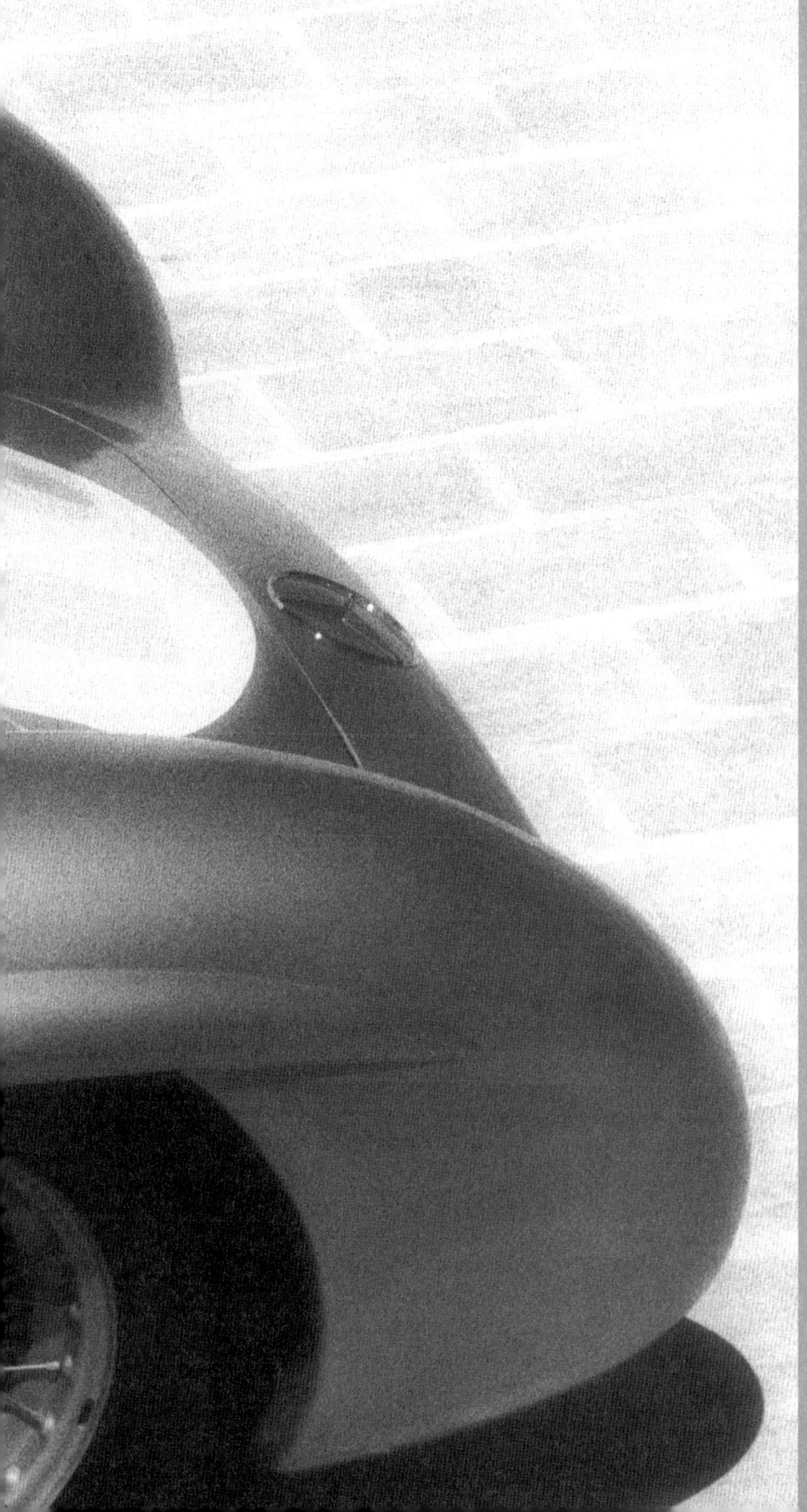

In 1954, the wind tunnel jointly owned by Mercedes-Benz and the Technical University of Stuttgart gave birth to a racing car of unique elegance. This original version of the W196, with its flawless streamlining and low air resistance, was set to sweep aside all competition. It did – but only on the fastest of circuits

W196

Aerodynamic design gave the Mercedes W196 its stature. With its sweeping body lines and a length of 4360 millimeters, it outclassed all its competitors

The attention to aerodynamic detail on the Mercedes W196 is painstaking. Cooling air flowing into the engine compartment is given an easy way out on either side

When Mercedes-Benz racing cars had long distances to cover in the 1950s, a racing transporter would be used. This low-loader from the research department had a top speed of 170 km/h, thanks to its engine borrowed from a Mercedes 300 SL

THE ARGENTINIAN'S
TWO MASTERPIECES

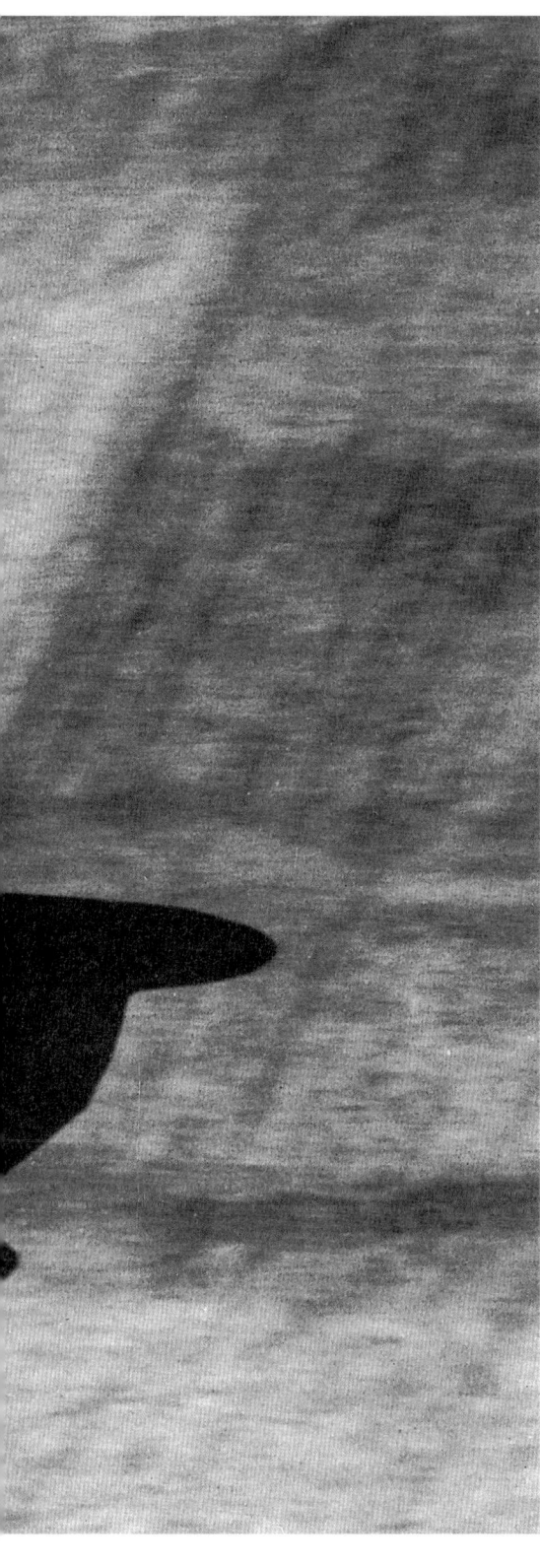

The Return of the Silver Arrows

July 4, 1954 brought a wonderful Sunday afternoon for Germans everywhere. The national football team faced the favorites Hungary in the final of the World Cup in Bern, a match they won in the dying seconds through an eighty-fourth-minute goal by Helmut Rahn. And whilst the majority of Germans were gathered around the radio following the football commentary with rapt attention, a second sporting contest – the French Grand Prix in Reims for the Formula One World Championships – was also underway and would soon be giving cause for further national celebration.

This was the third running of the event in Reims, although it was the first time with the Mercedes team taking part. Here, Mercedes was to meet head on the challenge thrown down by the classic monoposti of the opposing teams. With their new streamlined racing cars, the team from Stuttgart was soon able to underline its superiority on the fast Champagne circuit. Juan Manuel Fangio and Karl Kling finished well ahead of the rest of the field in their Mercedes W196.

That glorious afternoon for German sport provided a perfect accompaniment to other events of the period. The nation's fledgling republic had begun to strip away the grayness of the post-war years and the German economic miracle was just over the horizon. Daimler-Benz AG was well prepared. Topping its range once again was

In 1951 Juan Manuel Fangio was already back driving a Silver Arrow. With a 1939 Mercedes W154 he entered two races in Argentina

With the streamlined version of the Mercedes W196 Daimler-Benz made its return to Grand Prix motor racing in 1954. On fast, steeply banked circuits such as the Avus and the Autodromo at Monza, which at the time also had an oval track for Indianapolis cars, the Mercedes left the monoposti trailing in their wake

The 1950s | 77

Datum	Zeichnungs-Nr. V.-Nr	pro Lauf Km-Stand Einbau	Laufstrecke ges.	
27.6.54		ca. 20		1. Probelauf auf
30.6.54 u. 2.7.54		117	117	Training in Reim.
				Danach Zusatz-
4.7.54		500	617	Großer Preis von
				Wetter trocken, z
				Wagen das Renne
				Verbrauch = 46 L
12.7.54		ca. 20	617	Probelauf auf de
16.7.54		125	742	Training in Silvers
16.7.54			742	In Fahrerraum a
17.7.54		430	1172	Rennen in Silve
" "			1172	Beendete das R
" "			1172	Schnitt = 142,12 k
" "			1172	dann auch der
" "			1172	Karosserieschade
" "			1172	Verbrauch = 35 Lt
30.7.54		ca. 20	1172	Probelauf auf
31.7.54		97	1269	Training auf de
" "			1269	kühl. Rechten vora
1.8.54		502	1771	Rennen auf dem
" "			1771	Fahrer: Kling. Wett.
" "			1771	Rennen beendet
" "			1771	= 138 km/Std. In
" "			1771	achsträger die
" "			1771	Wurde an den B
" "			1771	aber sehr die Fa

Wagen-Nr. 196 R/3 Teil:

agement and Ludwig Kraus, who would later pursue his career with the Volkswagen Group.

The combined efforts of these four greats produced a racing car which – with the advantage of many years of hindsight – represented a remarkable blend of traditional engineering and bold progressive concepts.

Faced with an empty sheet of drawing paper in 1952, the team decided upon a wholly conventional front-engined car, despite the fact that the wild young constructors of the rapidly developing English racing scene were following a promising-looking trend towards designs incorporating a mid-engine.

But such decisions of fundamental design were not arrived without taking into account the overall engineering context: basic research still showed that an 8-cylinder offered

"the best of all worlds"

for a 2.5-liter racing engine – a fact which holds true even today.

The second issue concerned the approach to constructing the lightest 8-cylinder unit. Here, the design team considered the in-line engine more advantageous, since it required for its twin camshafts a single drive and not two as with the V-engine.

The disadvantage of the very long crankshaft was that it had a tendency towards torsional vibration under high load, but this was counteracted by dividing its effective length. The crankshaft of the straight-8 was composed of two 4-cylinder crankshafts with five anti-friction bearings. The power was transmitted via a gear assembly to a central drive shaft which in turn led to the transmission positioned behind the rear axle.

If the calculations were to be believed, this was the perfect concept for an engine. But because of its length and drive system, it was not one which would fit readily into a mid-sized motor car. In its fundamental design, the engine of the W196 – the Type M 196 – still bore remarkable similarities with the compressor powerhouses of the pre-war years. The cast steel cylinders with

Karl Kling and wife Vera were not the only ones to enjoy the sweet taste of victory after the first and successful race at Reims in 1954. The delight on the face of this unknown gendarme seems to suggest that entente cordiale was already well underway

Side-by-side, Fangio and Kling cross the finish line together in Reims in 1954. The foundation stone for a first World Championship has been laid

DAIMLER-BENZ AKTIENGESELLSCHAFT
STUTTGART-UNTERTÜRKHEIM

RENNVERTRAG

geschlossen zwischen Herrn Juan Manuel F A N G I O , Constitucion 1051, Buenos - Aires, Argentinien

und

der D A I M L E R - B E N Z Aktiengesellschaft, Stuttgart-Untertürkheim.

Die beiden Vertragsparteien treffen für das Jahr 1954 folgende Abmachungen:

1.) <u>Teilnahmeprogramm</u>

Herr Fangio verpflichtet sich, im Jahre 1954 für die Daimler-Benz AG folgende Veranstaltungen zu bestreiten:

a) <u>Sportwagenrennen</u>

12./13. Juni 1954	24-Stundenrennen von Le Mans
29. August 1954	1000 Kilometer auf dem Nürburgring
19.-23. November 1954	V. Carrera Panamericana "Mexico

b) <u>Rennwagenrennen</u>

4.7.1954	Großer Preis von Frankreich
17.7.1954	Großer Preis von England
1.8.1954	Großer Preis von Deutschland und Europa
22.8.1954	Großer Preis der Schweiz
5.9.1954	Großer Preis von Italien
26.9.1954	Avusrennen
24.10.1954	Großer Preis von Spanien

welded combustion chambers were bolted onto the light alloy crankcase, and once again the casing of the water jackets was made of a welded steel construction.

Where valve control was concerned, though, the development engineer Hans Gassmann set out on an entirely new and independent route. In his striving to achieve engine speed consistency, he was hoping to overcome one of the great obstacles associated with the four-stroke engine: its valve springs. Evidently the contemplative manner in which racing engine experts used to travel to work in 1952 played a part in helping Gassmann to come up with the solution to his problem. For it was whilst riding the tram one morning that he hit upon the idea of desmodromic valve control, or "Z control" (abbreviated from the German "Zwangssteuerung").

Fangio, Kling and Herrmann show their skill at formation flying on the Avus near Berlin in 1954. Kling won the race with an average speed of 213.5 km/h

He provided the racing engine's two overhead camshafts with a set of conventional cams to open the valves by means of mushroom tappets and then added a second set of cams to close the valves using rocker

Team boss Alfred Neubauer, seen here trackside on the left at the start/finish line at Reims, was bold enough to take charge of the stopwatch himself, suggesting that the spectacular first lap accidents we know from modern Formula One were in those days relatively unknown

Zu dieser Verpflichtung gehört auch die rechtzeitige Anwesenheit am Ort der Durchführung des Rennens. Die Anreise des Herrn Fangio hat nach den Weisungen der Rennleitung der DBAG zu erfolgen.

Die DBAG stellt ihrerseits Herrn Fangio für jedes Rennen am Rennort einen Sport- bzw. Rennwagen kostenlos zur Verfügung.

Alle mit der Teilnahme dieses Fahrzeugs und seiner Wartung verbundenen Auslagen, das heißt also insbesondere die Kosten für den An- und Abtransport, für den Betriebsstoff, für die Reifenerneuerung, sowie für die Kasko- und Haftpflichtversicherung, werden von der DBAG getragen. Letztere stellt auch die für die Betreuung notwendigen Mechaniker und ihre Rennorganisation für die Durchführung der Rennen.

Finanzielle Festlegungen

a) Vertragsabschlüsse mit den Veranstaltern

Alle Abmachungen mit den Veranstaltern hinsichtlich Teilnahme- und Prämienfragen führt die DBAG durch. Herr Fangio enthält sich solcher Abmachungen.

Das gleiche gilt für die Verhandlungen mit allen Zubehörteillieferanten der DBAG, betreffend alle Betriebsmittel, Reifen, sonstiges Zubehör, sowie Prämienfragen.

b) Startgeld

Das von den Veranstaltern für den jeweiligen Start bestimmte Startgeld wird Herrn Fangio von den Veranstaltern direkt ausbezahlt.

Für die beiden Rennen, für welche ein Startgeld seitens der Organisatoren nicht vorgesehen ist, also für das 24-Stundenrennen von Le Mans und die V. Carrera Panamericana "Mexico", legt die DBAG folgendes fest:

1. Für seinen Start beim 24-Stundenrennen von Le Mans erhält Herr Fangio US $ 1.200.- nach seiner Wahl entweder im offiziellen Zahlungsverkehr nach Argentinien oder den Gegenwert in deutscher oder französischer Währung. Dieses Startgeld wird Herrn Fangio unabhängig von seinen Erfolgsprämien ausbezahlt.

2. Für die Carrera Panamericana garantiert die DBAG Herrn Fangio eine Mindesteinnahme im Gegenwert von US $ 2.000.- (in Worten: Zweitausend US-Dollar). Falls die ihm zukommende Siegesprämie diese Summe nicht erreicht, wird ihm der Differenzbetrag bis zur Höhe von US $ 2.000.-- von der DBAG ausbezahlt.

c) Siegprämien

Bei Rennen, in welchen Herr Fangio das Fahrzeug allein steuert, erhält er alle vom Veranstalter ausgesetzten Geldprämien.

Muß Herr Fangio in einem Rennen durch einen Reservefahrer abgelöst werden, oder löst er einen anderen Hauptfahrer ab, so werden die von den betreffenden Fahrzeugen errungenen Geldpreise entsprechend den von den einzelnen Fahrern gefahrenen Rundenzahlen aufgeteilt. Für die vom Veranstalter aus irgendeinem Grunde nicht ausbezahlte Geldprämie ist die DBAG nicht ersatzpflichtig.

d) Prämien der Zubehörteilfirmen

Soweit seitens der DBAG mit den Zubehörteilfirmen Verträge abgeschlossen werden, die im Erfolgsfall die Auszahlung von Geldprämien an die Rennfahrer vorsehen, erhält Herr Fangio die auf ihn entfallenden Summen.

e) Von allen aus Punkten b, c und d auf Herrn Fangio entfallenden Startgelder, Sieggelder und sonstigen Prämien werden 10 % (Zehn Prozent) für die Rennorganisation in Abzug gebracht.

The relative prosperity of a World Champion in the 1950s did not come from the coffers of Daimler-Benz AG. At 1954 prices, the 1200 US-dollar appearance money for the 24-hour Le Mans race was less than the cost of a VW 1200. Considerably greater income was to be had in the form of premiums from the race organizers and from accessory manufacturers. Alfred Neubauer and the members of the racing organization received a ten per cent share of any drivers' earnings

f) Sollte sich aus irgendeinem Grunde der beabsichtigte Einsatz der DBAG bei einem der unter 1 a und b genannten Rennen nicht ermöglichen lassen, so geht Herr Fangio, der im übrigen bei allen Rennen eingesetzt wird, an denen sich die Daimler-Benz AG beteiligt, mindestens 3 Wochen vor der Veranstaltung darüber Mitteilung zu.

Für den Fall, daß die DBAG ein Rennen nicht beschicken kann, wird an Herrn Fangio eine Abstandssumme im Gegenwert von US $ 1.500.- pro Rennen bezahlt. Die Entscheidung, ob Herr Fangio es vorzieht, in einem solchen Fall mit einer anderen Firma eine Einzelabmachung abzuschließen oder ob er das Angebot der DBAG auf eine Abstandssumme von US $ 1.500.- pro Rennen annimmt, liegt auf Seiten des Herrn Fangio.

g) **Ehrenpreise**

Zufolge eines prinzipiellen Grundsatzes der DBAG fallen ihr alle Ehrenpreise zu, die als "Grose Länderpreise" bezeichnet werden. Dazu gehören auch die von einem Staatsoberhaupt gestifteten Preise.

Die DBAG behält sich vor, Herrn Fangio als Ersatz für diese Preise Erinnerungspreise an das jeweilige Rennen anfertigen zu lassen. Sonstige Preise, welche für den Fahrer bestimmt sind, erhält Herr Fangio.

) **Spesenabmachungen**

a) Die DBAG übernimmt im Jahr 1954 die Kosten für einen Flug des Herrn Fangio von Argentinien nach Europa und zurück über Mexico.

b) Die DBAG trägt alle Reisekosten des Herrn Fangio, die im Zusammenhang mit der Teilnahme an Rennen anfallen.

c) Für die Dauer der Rennen (einschl. An- und Abreise), des Trainings sowie für die Zeit, in der Versuchsfahrten durchgeführt werden, erhält Herr Fangio ein Taggeld im Gegenwert von US $ 20.---. Für den übrigen Aufenthalt des Herrn Fangio in Europa im Zusammenhang mit dem Rennprogramm, wird das Tagegeld im Gegenwert von US $ 15.-- festgesetzt.

Sollte nach 2 f Abs.2 Herr Fangio für eine andere Firma Rennen fahren, entfällt für die Dauer eines solchen Rennens einschließlich Trainingstage dieses Tagegeld.

Die Tagesspesen werden in der Währung des Landes zur Verfügung gestellt, in welchem sich Herr Fangio jeweils aufhält.

Versicherung

Die DBAG schließt für Herrn Fangio nach seiner Wahl in Deutschland oder Argentinien eine Unfallversicherung für das ganze Kalenderjahr 1954 ab. Die Höhen der Versicherungssummen sind bei Abschluss in Deutschland:

DM 100.000.-- für den Todesfall
DM 200.000.-- für den Invaliditätsfall
DM 50.-- Tagegeld
DM 10.000.-- Heilkosten

Bei Abschluss der Versicherung in Argentinien werden entsprechende Versicherungssummen unter Umrechnung auf der Basis des Kurses von 1 Peso = 0,30 DM festgesetzt.

Für diese Versicherungen haben die jeweils geltenden allgemeinen Versicherungsbedingungen Gültigkeit. Weitere Ansprüche irgendwelcher Art kann Herr Fangio wegen eines Unfalles gegen die DBAG nicht erheben. Die Versicherung gilt nicht für den Fall und die Zeit, für die Herr Fangio mit einer anderen Firma Abmachungen trifft.

Leihwagen

Während der Zeit seines Aufenthaltes in Europa im Zusammenhang mit Aufgaben für die DBAG erhält Herr Fangio einen Leihwagen unseres Bauprogramms, und zwar entweder einen Typ 220 oder einen Typ 300.

The fact that Juan Manuel Fangio received 1500 US-dollars for a race he did not take part in – in other words, more than the usual appearance fee – was the result of compensation paid to him for lost premiums. The single return flight to Argentina per year, paid for by his employers, might also seem rather parsimonious. But the agreed daily expenses in the mid-1950s did not mean the drivers went hungry. One dollar was equivalent to four Deutschmarks – and a good square meal in a restaurant rarely cost more than ten of those

6.) Standort des Herrn Fangio in Europa

Die Wahl des Standortes in Europa während einer Wartezeit von Rennen zu Rennen wird Herrn Fangio freigestellt.

7.) Engagement anderer Fahrer

Herrn Fangio wird zugesichert, daß im Rennjahr 1954 kein weiterer argentinischer Fahrer bei der Mercedes-Benz-Rennmannschaft eingesetzt wird.

8.) Gerichtsstand

Dieser Vertrag ist in deutscher und spanischer Sprache abgefaßt. Im Falle von Streitigkeiten gilt der deutsche Text. Gerichtsstand ist Stuttgart.

9.) Sämtliche Zahlungen, die die DBAG an Herrn Fangio zu leisten hat, erfolgen unter Beachtung der deutschen und gegebenenfalls auch der argentinischen Devisenbestimmungen. Gegenwärtiger Vertrag bedarf noch der Genehmigung der deutschen Devisenbehörde; die DBAG verpflichtet sich, diese Genehmigung unverzüglich zu beantragen.

Zur Sicherung eines reibungslosen Ablaufes der Veranstaltungen und des sportlichen Erfolges wird Herr Fangio allen Anweisungen der DB-Rennleitung Folge leisten.

Buenos-Aires, den 30. Maerz 1954

Stuttgart-Untertürkheim, den 27. Februar 1954

....
(Juan Manuel Fangio)

Daimler-Benz Aktiengesellschaft

In the 1950s streamlined body shells were still permitted in Formula One; today, however, regulations allow only open wheels

arms. The form-locking valve train without free-moving masses encouraged Gassmann to experiment with larger and heavier valves. As a result he moved away from the four-valve design hitherto preferred by Mercedes and made do instead with two large valves (intake 50 mm, exhaust 43 mm) per cylinder. By restricting the number of valves to two, the engineers discovered an interesting advantage: it created room for the two spark plugs needed for dual ignition.

The architecture of the cylinder head was dramatically at variance with what had been the norm at Mercedes. The inlet ducts followed a straight line running between the camshafts to the intake valves. This solution was clearly also part of the same endeavor that resulted in the engine being inclined sharply at 53 degrees – that of keeping the form of the drive assembly as low as possible so as to achieve low wind resistance.

Before building the 8-cylinder in its entirety, the racing department prepared a single-cylinder engine which exhibited all the essential dimensions of the later race engine – a 76 mm bore and 68.8 mm stroke, giving 312 cm³ for one cylinder and 2496 cm³ for all eight. Initial output tests were carried out with the single-cylinder engine, experimenting of course with the valve control times and other parameters. This approach to using a

"single-cylinder test engine"

is regarded as standard practice even fifty years on. At Ilmor, engine suppliers to McLaren-Mercedes, remarkably similar single-cylinder test engines are still used today. They may have a slightly reduced volume – 299 cm³ rather than 312 cm³, but in one particular respect they differ significantly: the maximum speed of the crankshaft has increased from 8000 to 18,000 or more revolutions per minute.

The revolutionary innovation in the race engine was direct fuel injection. Bosch built a special eight-chamber high-pressure pump which fed gasoline at a pressure of 85 bar directly through the cylinder wall and angled upwards into the combustion chamber during the induction stroke.

In 1954 the fuel concoction injected was not a particularly healthy mix for anyone to get too close to.

But the cocktail of 45 per cent benzol, 25 per cent methyl alcohol, 25 per cent aviation fuel, three per cent acetone and two per cent nitrobenzol certainly seemed to boost output. The Mercedes M 196 race engine developed 290 hp at 8500 rpm, bettering all its rivals during the period.

Most motorists in Germany had cars with rather fewer horsepower to get from A to B. The VW Beetle, for example, had just been given a 30 hp engine. At the bottom end of the Mercedes range, which had rather

In 1955 it was Stirling Moss who drove the number sixteen car at Monza, pictured here entering the banked curve

unexpectedly adopted the fashionable three-box body after years of traditional design, was the 180 Diesel with 40 hp. And the Porsche 1500 Super was about as good as it got with 70 hp. But only a minority of Germans actually owned a car. With just 1.3 million passenger cars for the country as a whole, theoretical car sharing worked out at roughly one vehicle for every fifty people. And that at a time when the labor force was working almost a 49-hour week. Worldwide, the number of automobiles had by this time risen to 100 million, of which 60 per cent were in the USA. Here, statistics reveal that the average American was still only working approximately 40 hours per week.

It would be interesting to know whether a certain Elvis Presley stuck to the regulation 40 hours or not. He was just 19 years old in 1954, and stood at the start of a unique career as charismatic rock'n'roll singer and film actor, though with no thoughts of Oscars as yet.

And at the same time in America a new develop-

Juan Manuel Fangio in Monza in 1954. The track still had cobblestones in places; nowadays there are escape lanes where once spectators used to stand. Showing little concern for their own safety, photographers and marshals enjoyed their privileged, if risky, trackside position

Two generations of Mercedes W196 are pictured inside a covered truck. By summer 1954 the monoposto had begun to take over from the "streamlined" car

ment was already gleaming on the horizon – disk brakes. Chrysler had borrowed them from the aviation industry as early as 1950 – tail-fins by this time, too. The Mercedes-Benz W196 racing car was to be one of the last and most remarkable to feature drum brakes. In order to reduce unsprung masses, the engineers removed all four drums from the wheels and mounted them inside the car. With the rear brakes, the deceleration experts followed a tried-and-tested approach. Drums were positioned close to the differential, and braking power was transmitted via the existing propshafts of the drive system. At the front, the brake system and the two drums were mounted in the space frame in front of the engine; the rest followed more or less the same principle as at the rear, using two propshafts dedicated to the transmission of braking power.

There was even initial consideration paid to the notion of using this existing design for a four-wheel drive in order to improve traction from the start in first gear. But it was clear enough that even without this additional investment the car was pretty quick off the mark when the flag went down.

The drum brakes had a respectable diameter (front 350 mm, rear 275 mm) and the brake-shoes were enormously wide (90 m). Built into each brake were

"eight wheel brake cylinders",

whose job it was to press the heavy brake-shoes with the necessary force against the drum.

Rudolf Uhlenhaut was careful to get the correct geometry for the wheel suspension. Long double wishbones at the front axle; at the rear, however, design of the running gear returned to the principle of the swing axle, although its central fulcrum was positioned well below the differential and the output of the drive shafts. This configuration solved most of the disadvantages of the swing axle. Changes in camber were reduced, positive camber was eradicated and a stop was put to the unweighting effect of the outside wheel on cornering.

Torsion bars took over the job of providing suspension in the W196, and by this time, of course, there were ribbed telescopic shock absorbers. In 1954 the trend in international body shell design was towards a three-box body shape with just a discreet hint of fender. This styling was a feature picked up by the original version of the W196, its all-round streamlined body contrasting starkly with the conventional open-wheeled racing cars. The elegant lines of the W196, no longer permitted in Formula One, were developed in-house in the Mercedes wind tunnel with the clearly defined aim of cutting drag to make the car even faster.

Such calculations were found to be accurate on the fast circuit at Reims. But even Fangio had trouble with this broad-beamed racer on the winding Silverstone course. He rammed the oil drums bordering the edge of the circuit and wrote off the body. Somewhat embarrassed by this performance, the Mercedes team redoubled its efforts to produce a genuine open-wheeled monoposto in time for the German Grand Prix on the Nürburgring.

The Eifel race proved that the relative superiority

Lined up in the drivers' enclosure, an elegant cut above the rest, the aerodynamic Mercedes W196 proudly displays the enclosed bodywork of a sports car

The slender racer had its premiere at the Nürburgring. Fangio is here seen leading Moss and Lang. Herrmann is behind Lang, struggling with the "streamlined" version

of the new Mercedes cars was nothing without the energetic involvement of their drivers. On the first lap, the Ferrari driver José Froilan Gonzalez succeeded in showing his countryman Fangio and the rest of the field a clean pair of heels. The fact that Fangio finally regained the lead had as much to do with his skilful driving as with the car's performance.

Similarly, Fangio won the Italian Grand Prix in Monza not because his Mercedes was a superior car, but because he drove it sparingly from start to finish. During the first half of the race, brake problems had left him in a seemingly hopeless position behind Stirling Moss in the Maserati and Alberto Ascari in the Ferrari. But Ascari retired, and on the final lap Moss' engine seized. He ended up pushing the Maserati over the finish to salvage tenth position. Fangio congratulated Moss as the race's moral victor – it was to be the start of long-lasting friendship.

From a German perspective – having become World Champions in football and Formula One in the same year – the world seemed a friendly place in 1955. With the ratification of the Treaty of Paris, the rule of occupying armies had come to an end. Now there was the prospect of Germany forming part of a European union, and just ten years after the end of the war the Federal Republic was taking its first steps towards joining NATO. The German Lufthansa reopened a limited number of scheduled services, leaving other airlines to compete for the incredible 27-hour Copenhagen – Los Angeles route via the North Pole. Much more down-to-earth were the events in the world of the silver screen at the time. "La Strada" was the name of Federico Fellini's film starring Giulietta Masina and Anthony Quinn, the darling of the cinema-going public.

In 1955 some of the Mercedes cars were modified slightly for Formula One use. The wheelbase was shortened to improve maneuverability. As a result, space at the front of the car was in short supply and the drum brakes had to be mounted outboard. In addition, Daim-

Even at its first outing on the Nürburgring in 1954, the slimline Mercedes W196 "monoposto" showed its superior class. Fangio, pictured here in the lead, was eventually able to secure a comfortable victory over his pursuer Kling

In 1954 it was still possible to photograph the start of the Swiss Grand Prix in Bremgarten near Bern in close-up

ler-Benz AG doubled its involvement in motor sport, following a principle one would today refer to as a platform strategy. During the course of the winter, the Formula One racing cars had provided the engineering basis for a sports car – a two-seater, but nevertheless very close in looks to the streamlined racers.

The 300 SLR sports car had a similar space frame, the same drive concept, but the engine had a longer stroke – its 78 mm bore and 78 mm stroke giving a 2980 cm³ displacement. Output reached a maximum of 310 hp – not quite as big an increase as shown in the displacement, since the engine ran on standard fuel.

For one of the *formule libre* races in Argentina there was even a hybrid version – a monoposto with 3-liter engine.

The Formula One field during the 2.5-liter era threw up quite a variety of engines for Mercedes to compete against. Ferrari's hopes rested with their Type 625, a lightweight 4-cylinder which developed 265 hp at 7200 rpm. Lancia's relatively short guest appearance on the Formula One stage was with a V8 engine which in 1954 had produced 260 hp at 8000 rpm. The 6-cylinder in-line Maserati unit achieved the same figures. But it was the 315 hp at 10,000 rpm of Maserati's V12 engine which defined the boundaries for such increases in power – though it would be nine years before it was properly put through its paces. The technical diversity which characterized Formula One in the 1950s would never be seen to the same degree again.

In the 1955 season Fangio found himself alongside ambitious competition: Stirling Moss, the moral victor from Monza, was now driving for Mercedes. The 1955 season thus became a

"duel between friends".

On May 1 Moss/Jenkinson won the Mille Miglia in the 300 SLR in a record time ahead of the solo driver Fangio. But on May 29 "El Chueco" struck back with a victory in the Eifel race on the Nürburgring – Fangio took first place in the Mercedes 300 SLR, Moss was runner-up in the same car.

The final race tally between the two Mercedes drivers stood at 7:4 in Fangio's favor, and with that he became World Champion for the third time. Stirling

Awards ceremony 1954. After the Swiss Grand Prix a young soap-box racer has the honor of presenting his grown-up colleagues with an entire round of Emmental cheese. As Kling and Fangio seem less than excited by the homemade homage, other team members can confidently look forward to a generous portion of the Swiss specialty

Moss entered the motor racing history books as the most successful driver never to win an individual World Championship title, but his victory at the Targa Florio in Sicily ensured that Mercedes-Benz also became the 1955 Sports Car World Champions.

One thing the two rivals were never given was the chance to win a race together. They did, however, come close to achieving this at the 24-hour Le Mans race. As they took it in turns at the wheel of their Mercedes SLR, they gradually increased their lead over the rest of the field. Then, suddenly, disaster struck. A driving error from an opponent caused the Mercedes 300 SLR of Frenchman Pierre Levegh to spin off into one of the stands, killing the driver and 82 spectators.

Alfred Neubauer later ordered all his cars to quit the race, and at the end of the season Daimler-Benz AG withdrew from motor sport altogether for a lengthy period – their absence from Formula One was to be even longer.

That year, 1955, an Elia Kazan film starring James Dean and Julie Harris hit the box offices from America – "East of Eden" was to become the cult classic of a new generation. But the film also threw some light, perhaps, on the Stuttgart company's decision to quit racing.

Left-hand page: Pictured here at Monaco in 1955, Stirling Moss swings the monoposto version of the Mercedes W196 through Gasometer Corner with appreciable side-tilt

Even in 1954 technical problems could lead to lively discussion. Alfred Neubauer is pictured here defending his point vigorously

Elegant trees still lined the circuit in Monaco in 1955. And despite the familiar bunching at the start, the cars, too, seem a world away. World Champion Fangio has taken up the strategically more favorable position on the inside against Stirling Moss

By the summer of 1954, in time for the German Grand Prix, the slimmed down version of the Mercedes W196, the "monoposto" appeared at the Nürburgring's Nordschleife. This classically-styled Grand Prix racing car with free-standing wheels was no longer as aerodynamic – the drag coefficient rose from 0.43 to 0.62 – but the car was more compact and appreciably better on winding circuits. To improve handling still further, the wheelbase was shortened in 1955 from 2350 to 2150 millimeters

The tubular space frame was modeled on the streamlined Mercedes 300 SL and used in the "monoposto" with little modification. The gear lever for the five-speed transmission and everything that went with it reveals engineering from a bygone age

W196

The Mercedes W196 "monoposto" could not boast the sleekest of body shells, because the 8-cylinder engine lies almost flat under the front of the hood. With a capacity of 265 liters, the tank at the rear is the chef d'oeuvre of a craftsman with complete mastery of the art of welding aluminum

The 1950s | 99

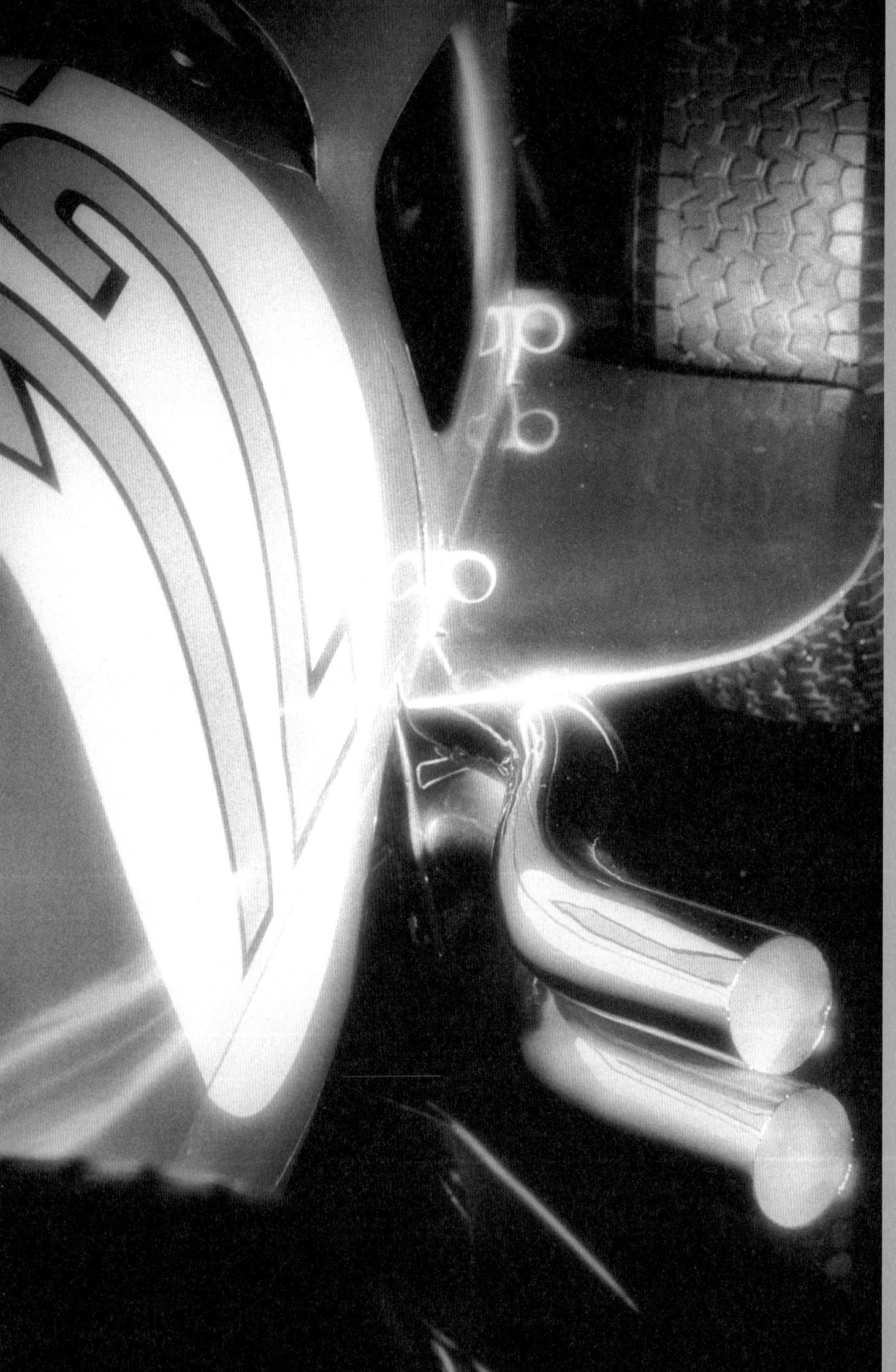

The fins behind the front wheels were aerodynamic aids with a rather unusual function back in 1954. They were designed to protect the driver's face from spray in the event of rain during a race

The 1950s | 105

Juan Manuel Fangio

Juan Manuel Fangio dominated the Grand Prix racing scene of the 1950s in a way nobody had done before, winning five World Championships and, in the process, setting a record which would probably never be broken. Fifty years ago he took over where the generation of "gentleman racers" had left off.

Only rarely has Juan Manuel Fangio been photographed looking so ill-humored. By nature he was full of exuberance – "El Chueco" with bandy legs. It is not just silky driving skills which he had in common with Michael Schumacher, but also a talent for football

Appearances can be deceptive, however. Juan Manuel was born on June 24, 1911. He was 40 by the time of his first world title in 1951 – so not much younger than the Mercedes works drivers of the 1930s. Former champion Caracciola was ten years his senior, von Brauchitsch only six.

Along with many other Italians, his grandfather Giuseppe Fangio emigrated to Argentina in the nineteenth century, settling in the small town of Balcarce in the country's interior. He began work as a charcoal burner in the local grill restaurants known as *parillas* and *lomotecas*. Evidently he was good at his job: with the money he was able to put away, he bought twenty-five acres of land on the outskirts of Balcarce as security for the rest of the family, who could now also leave Italy for Argentina.

This was how Juan Manuel's father Don Loreto Fangio came to South America. Having taken a job in Balcarce as a stonemason, he saved every penny and bought a plot of land to construct a modest house of his own. Before long, however, the house would need an extension, for Don Loreto had found a wife – an Italian girl in Argentina by the name of Herminia – with whom he settled down and had six children.

Life was not particularly easy for the offspring of immigrant families at the turn of the century, as Juan Manuel Fangio's accounts reveal all too clearly. Whilst still at school he was sent by his father to do an apprenticeship with a local blacksmith, where he was soon working seven days a week.

A career in motor racing had not entered the young Fangio's head at this stage. Any free moments he had were devoted – as one might expect from an Italo-Argentinian – to the school football team. The other players called him

"El Chueco"

a nickname meaning "bandy legs", which was to stick with him for the rest of his life. When the town's blacksmith left Balcarce, Fangio started helping out in car repair shops. He left school at the end of the sixth grade, aged twelve, in order to train as a motor mechanic. This decision was to change the course of his life, for he found an apprenticeship at the Studebaker dealership run by Miguel Viggiano, himself a racing driver and responsible for looking after Manuel Ayerza's racing cars – a big name in the sport in Argentina at the time.

Inevitably Juan got involved in the racing side of things. When he reached 18, he was chosen by Manuel Ayerza to assist him as co-driver in a gravel-track race in a Chevrolet, and the following year he did the same for his brother-in-law Bruja Font in a Plymouth on the La Chata racing circuit near Balcarce.

Before he could take control in the cockpit himself, however, he was obliged to do his statutory two years' military service. As soon as this was completed in 1932, he set up a car repair shop on his father's land with a friend from the football club, José Duffard. They gave it the name "Fangio, Duffard y Cia."

Fangio certainly did not regard the repair shop as a quick way to get involved in racing. He was not to compete in his first race until 1936. For this event he borrowed a taxi from friends, removed the heavy and capacious bodyshell from the chassis and replaced it with the minimum

The 1950s | 107

required for two people. The race itself brought neither victory nor any hoped-for prize money. Instead the customized taxi went home with big-end bearing damage which had to be fixed at the workshops of "Fangio, Duffard y Cia."

A subsequent start – this time in his own 1934 Ford with a 1938 V8 engine – also failed to achieve the breakthrough he hoped for. Fangio soon learned that dirt from the rough Argentinian tracks was at its thickest when thrown up from the rear wheels of his faster opponents. But after a dozen or more races the dust gradually began to settle and Fangio moved up towards the front of the pack.

Such doggedness on the part of the now 28-year-old Juan Manuel Fangio must have appealed to the good townsfolk of Balcarce – they started collecting money on his behalf for a new competition-standard racing car. Failing to get hold of a V8 Ford in time, their choice fell on a Chevrolet coupe with the 6-cylinder "Blue Flame" engine.

In 1939 Fangio finished fifth in the Gran Premio Argentino and thirteenth in the national 1000-km Tour of Argentina. But that elusive place on the world stage was still not quite within his grasp.

Things were on the up in 1940. The automobile club of Argentina organized the Gran Premio Internacional del Norte, a 9500-km road race which started in Buenos Aires, ran up through the Andes, crossing Bolivia to Lima in Peru before returning to the finish in the Argentinian capital.

For Fangio there was just one problem – he had no car. To raise funds, his friends in Balcarce this time organized a tombola with one prize only: an almost mint condition 1940 Chevrolet. Although the winner had to wait until after the race to take possession of his prize, the audacious plan worked and Fangio had his first major success. He won the Gran Premio and became Argentinian champion both in that year and the one to follow.

From now on, it was Juan Manuel Fangio's turn to leave all his opponents trailing in the South American dust. He had become a figure of national importance. But in 1942 racing matters came to an abrupt end. Argentina also became subject to the fuel rationing imposed as a result of the Second World War.

Fangio soon found reason to appreciate his

"natural ability"

as a salesman. During the war years he dealt in tires, and after the war was over he turned to American army surplus trucks. But when motor racing started up in Argentina again, "El Chueco" came out of retirement and went back to his life on the racing circuit and in the workshops.

"Negrita" was the name he gave to another audacious automobile project – affectionately named for its coat of black paint. Among its more unusual identifying features were the Model-T Ford chassis and the 3.9-liter 6-cylinder engine borrowed from a relatively recent Chevrolet. At the

Fangio's unmistakable charm guaranteed a string of attractive female admirers. In 1954 it was never too late for an opportunistic flirt on the circuit before practice

wheel of this machine, Fangio thundered after the European racing elite, recently arrived in Argentina to take part in the Temporada race series at the invitation of the automobile club. But by 1948 even this opportunity was no longer available to him. Negrita & Co, cars classified as *mecánica nacional*, were barred from entering the race; in future, only genuine Grand Prix cars would be permitted to appear in Temporada races. But the Automobile Club of Argentina had hinted that it would make appropriate cars available to qualified drivers.

Juan Manuel Fangio applied for such a car to the chairman of the motor sport committee Don Francesco Borgonovo. Sadly, there is no record of what language the two spoke – Spanish or Italian –, but the outcome of the conversation was clear: Fangio would get a Maserati 4CL, a pre-war 1.5-liter voiturette and then later the fragile 1100 Gordini. Success did not come readily.

The Automobile Club of Argentina was looking to do more than just breathe life into the domestic racing scene, however. Don Francesco Borgonovo was still determined to have Argentinian drivers contesting Grand Prix races in Europe. It is possible that President Juan Domingo Perón with spouse Evita helped to realize this notion, embracing it with dictatorial zeal. In any case, the club decided to invest in the necessary racing cars.

Fangio was sent to Italy with a delegation to find and purchase the right car. He chose the latest Maserati 4CLT/48 – one of the new, smaller generation of Grand Prix cars, whose 1.5 liter 4-cylinder engine with a four-valve design developed 260 hp thanks to its two-stage compressor.

"With this Maserati"

Fangio won five Grand Prix races in 1949, four in Europe and one in Argentina. He considered his greatest victory to be his Formula Two win at Monza, since it was here that he beat the two Ferrari works drivers Alberto Ascari and Luigi Villoresi in his Ferrari Tipo 166 F, also paid for out of Argentinian state coffers.

The win possibly also secured Juan Manuel Fangio a contract as a works driver in the Formula One team with Alfa Romeo in 1950. Three wins were not quite enough to clinch the overall title, however, and he ended the season runner-up behind teammate Giuseppe Farina.

As early as 1950 the Mercedes-Benz team manager Alfred Neubauer had started making approaches to this rising talent from Argentina. He signed Fangio up for two races on home soil – Fangio's readiness to accept showing his love of attempting the impossible. For in that Argentinian winter of 1951 Fangio would be racing the now twelve-year-old Mercedes W154. The 3-liter compressor was far from its peak form, nevertheless Fangio managed to take third place following a retirement in the first race.

At the end of the 1951 season, however, it was his points total as an Alfa Romeo works driver which counted, and he took his first World Championship title after just three years in Grand Prix motor racing.

After two back-to-back world titles, Alfa Romeo decided to end its involvement in Formula One and Fangio initially returned to South America in 1952, where he spruced up his old Ferrari, the Tipo 166 F 2,

Even during the build-up to the start of the 1955 Mille Miglia, Fangio still finds time to share a joke. Neither the enthusiast eager to offer his goggles, nor the lady casting soulful looks in her hero's direction, can put the champion off his stride

winning six races during the course of the southern hemisphere winter.

An invitation to race in Europe again from April 1952 onwards ended tragically in June that year. He started the Monza Grand Prix in a 2-liter Maserati, the A6GCM, but an error on lap two led to a serious accident going into the Lesmo bend. The Maserati flipped over and Fangio was thrown from the car. His survival was attributed to the regulation crash helmet he was wearing; nevertheless, he was to spend the next three months in traction with several cracked vertebrae.

But Fangio was soon back looking for new adventure. In 1953 – never one to shy away from possible failure – "El Chueco" climbed aboard the BRM Formula One car. With its 1.5-liter 16-cylinder engine delivering a peak output of 450 hp, this was the most powerful engine of its time.

But after three retirements the BRM was showing the unpredictable nature of its arcane engineering. And yet a second place for Fangio demonstrated the sensitive way in which he was able to coax the best out of even the most temperamental of cars.

"A contract"

with Maserati in 1953 made him the darling of the Italians, since he drove to victory at both the autodromo at Modena and in the park in Monza. He also became the hero of the Mille Miglia that year in an Alfa Romeo Disco Volante. Fangio was forced to complete the second half of the long distance classic with steering so defective he could barely guide the car around the corners – and yet he still managed to salvage second place.

Fangio concluded the 1953 season with a very convincing win at the Carrera Panamericana in Mexico in November driving a Lancia. But the year ended without a further title.

All this was to change in 1954, however. A new Formula One was introduced and Fangio's second World Championship season began with a home win at the autodromo in Buenos Aires, although these were not yet points he was earning for Mercedes. Until Rudolf Uhlenhaut's W196 was ready, Fangio remained a works driver for Maserati and went on to take a

The Mercedes-Benz team in 1955: Piero Taruffi, Juan Manuel Fangio, Karl Kling, Alfred Neubauer, Stirling Moss and André Simon. The injured Hans Herrmann was unfortunately not present

second victory with the new Type 250 F at the Belgian Grand Prix in Spa-Francorchamps.

"His winning streak"

for Mercedes-Benz did not start until midway through the year in Reims, France. He won here on July 4 and notched up three further victories to take a second world title in 1954.

The World Champion's diary for 1955 soon filled up. In all, he competed in five title races for the Formula One championship, clinching the title for a third time, and drove the Mercedes 300 SLR in six sports car events. At the Mille Miglia that year he finished second – without a co-driver – behind the 300 SLR of Stirling Moss and Denis Jenkinson.

When Daimler-Benz AG withdrew from motor racing in 1955, Juan Manuel Fangio continued his winning ways. He became World Champion on two further occasions: in 1956 with Lancia-Ferrari and in 1957 with Maserati. That made five world titles in total, four of them in succession – a feat which will probably never be matched by any Formula One driver.

After his last race – the 1958 French Grand Prix in Reims – Juan Manuel Fangio decided to return to once again to the world of commerce. He became President of Mercedes-Benz Argentina, a role he carried out unstintingly and to great effect until his death from kidney failure on July 17, 1995.

Juan Manuel Fangio was unquestionably the superior competitor when matched against his colleagues at Mercedes-Benz, but Karl Kling and the rest of the team valued the friendship of the exuberant Argentinian enormously

Football is not the only sport where the top teams make good use of their wings

The steering wheel in contemporary Formula One racing cars is no longer circular but butterfly-shaped. With its array of buttons it looks more like a control module for a computer game

As a result of the wind tunnel, modern racing cars have wings all over. But regulations oblige designers to position wings at fixed distances from one another, in order to reduce negative lift and cornering speed

Surrounding air is also used to increase the smooth operation of the 10-cylinder engine hidden some way back behind the driver and the fuel tank. The large opening above the driver's headrest sucks air in at a carefully regulated boost pressure

Mercedes-Benz files its racing history in made-to-measure container shelving. Here in a motoring microclimate, Mika Hakkinen's 1998 World Championship car is kept safe and dry with some of its relatives, awaiting an appearance in the museum or a chance to clear its throat at a classic car event

Forty-four years – and a wholly new approach to aerodynamic design – separate the streamlined Mercedes W196 from the McLaren Mercedes of today. In the past, a few hours in the wind tunnel was considered enough to reduce air resistance adequately. Nowadays a great deal more time and effort is invested in achieving perfectly counterbalanced negative lift

With their noses in the air, Formula One cars of the 90s had a rather haughty appearance. But the racing business is about designing efficiency not beauty

MP4/13

SILVER MAKES A COMEBACK WITH WEST

Silver Arrows – the third coming

The third Silver Arrow era proved to be a long time coming and was something of a cloak and dagger affair in the early years. It was with a discreet return to motor racing in mind that Mercedes-Benz was prepared to allow Dr. Rudolf Hörnig to begin testing on a jet-heeled version of the 5-liter, 8-cylinder engine fitted with twin turbochargers. At last, this was the spark to ignite the Group C sports cars run by Swiss team owner Peter Sauber.

"We didn't want our activities to be common knowledge within the plant," admits Board member Jürgen Hubbert, "it was all a kind of moonlighting, if you like."

With Sauber's improved performance and increasing success, Dr. Hörnig's "undercover testing" took on a new legitimacy. Sponsorship from Daimler-Benz subsidiary AEG strengthened the bond between the racing cars – still dark blue at the time – and the Mercedes-Benz brand. In 1990, at the end of a promising season and with the reunification of Germany now sealed, a voice of decree rang out from within the Group. It was Head of Mercedes-Benz Werner Niefer who gave the order: "Next year, the cars will be painted silver."

The Silver Arrows were back, but they had yet to

According to rule changes introduced in 1998, a Formula One car may not measure more than 1800 mm in width from one rear tire sidewall to the other. When measured in the same way, the most powerful DaimlerChrysler Group sports car, the Viper, exceeds these dimensions

Ron Dennis, Mika Hakkinen, Jürgen Hubbert, David Coulthard, Norbert Haug and the rest of the team have good reason to celebrate at the end of their fourth season in partnership: in 1998 Hakkinen drove his McLaren Mercedes to the World Championship title for the first time

reclaim their rightful place on the top step of the Formula One podium. However, that is exactly where many within Mercedes-Benz wanted to see them, to inject new verve into a company which had grown somewhat ponderous on the fruits of prosperity. Board member Werner Niefer and technical director Jürgen Hubbert were active supporters of the plan to build a new Mercedes in the image of its illustrious predecessors. The proposal was put to the Board for discussion and subsequently rejected – a decision in line with the strategy pursued by Group Chairman Edzard Reuter and supported by Werner Niefer. Motor sport was to remain an afterthought in the eyes of the company.

Mercedes' involvement in the Sports Car World Championship came to end in 1992 and Peter Sauber's team moved up to Formula One, their V10 engines displaying the words "powered by Mercedes-Benz". That this was possible at all was thanks to a business deal between two friends – US businessman and racing team manager Roger Penske and Helmut Werner, who had taken over the helm at Mercedes-Benz after Niefer's death. Penske held a 25 per cent stake in the recently established British racing engine manufacturer Ilmor Engineering, with company founders

"Mario Illien and Paul Morgan"

each retaining 25 per cent. The remaining quarter was acquired by Chevrolet, a customer at the time. However, the American car giant was looking to pull out of Indy-car racing and sell its share. That was when Penske drew the attention of his friend Werner to a potential opportunity for Mercedes and had Werner reaching for his check book.

Mercedes-Benz supplied the Sauber team with Ilmor Formula One engines for two years, but the burning desire to be back at the top soon led to talks with the leading teams. Jürgen Hubbert and motor sport boss Norbert Haug entered into negotiations not just with McLaren, but also with the Williams team and the motor sport impresario Tom Walkinshaw, who had enjoyed success across a range of categories.

McLaren team principal Ron Dennis had experience of working with German partners, and this was to be to his benefit during the negotiations. His record included world championship titles won with TAG engines from Porsche, and production of the McLaren-BMW Formula One super sports car victorious at Le Mans. "Of all the Europeans, the Germans share the greatest similarities with the English, and that makes the partnership a harmonious one," confirmed Ron Dennis. In 1995, the Silver Arrows returned at last to Grand Prix racing with McLaren, 40 years after Mercedes-Benz had last won the Formula One World Championship.

The international McLaren Mercedes team, including drivers Mika Hakkinen from Finland and Englishman Nigel Mansell, was unveiled in celebratory fashion at the British Museum in London.

Hakkinen had already made himself comfortable behind the wheel of his McLaren, but Mansell did not

Monaco's crash barriers provide a silver frame for Mika Hakkinen, as he drives his Silver Arrow to a maiden victory in the principality

In Formula One the circuits visited during the course of a season are as varied as the girls who hold up the start numbers on the grid

stay for long – the 1992 World Champion (in a Williams) waved goodbye after the Spanish Grand Prix. Another British driver, Mark Blundell, took over until the end of the season.

In 1995 all things Scottish were flavor of the month in the media, following Australian actor Mel Gibson's portrayal of a Scottish freedom warrior in the Hollywood film "Braveheart". The epic story of the courageous highlander who led his people in an uprising against the English 700 years ago was awarded an Oscar by the Academy of Motion Picture Arts and Sciences in the category Best Film. McLaren Mercedes found their own Scotsman in 1996, luring David Coulthard from Williams-Renault to partner Mika Hakkinen.

After riding a steep learning curve in the first season back, McLaren Mercedes' fortunes improved only slightly the following year. Things had changed in Formula One and radical technical concepts did not provide an easy route back to past successes. For McLaren boss Ron Dennis, among others, this was a source of some regret: "I certainly envy the engineers and designers of the past, who could really go to town technically and build wonderful cars to win races. And even if they didn't win, failure was much more glorious than it is today."

But maybe the team managers of yesteryear would also have reason to envy Ron Dennis – and not just for the eleven Drivers' and eight Constructors' World Championship titles McLaren have notched up. Dennis once enlisted the Spice Girls to put the visual and acoustic icing on his presentation of a new Formula One generation. When it comes to the racing, it isn't just the official result that counts. Indeed, in the pecking order of today's racing elite, the team which can tap the most from the rich and beautiful in the VIP lounge comes out on top.

Since 1998, David Coulthard and Mika Hakkinen have made themselves at home at the head of the field. The Ilmor-built Mercedes engine has become one of the most powerful in Formula One

Mika Hakkinen cuts a totally absorbed figure as he gazes skywards. It is a typical pose in the breaks during qualifying, as the drivers analyze the progress of their rivals on the overhead monitors

Technical advances in the second half of the 1990s were conspicuous only by their virtual absence. Inching its way forward, technology in Formula One proved that Charles Darwin's theory of the evolution of species is also true of mechanical creatures. Indeed, the diversity which blossomed to such dazzling effect 40 years previously has been followed by the standardization inevitable as nature and technology get ever closer to the perfect form.

Formula One regulations have played an active role in promoting this development. Exotic engines have long since been banned. Aerodynamic aids are strictly limited in their form and effect. Clearly defined dimensions are stipulated for both the cars and their tires. And the all-powerful electronics systems have been put firmly in their place: anti-lock braking systems are outlawed (after all, good drivers should know how to brake), as are driving dynamics control systems (in general, there are no moose to avoid). The most important tasks of the designers and engineers now involve extremely precise work on areas of detail and in achieving

"absolute perfection".

However, in the world of career perfectionists the first win can be a long time coming, even with a healthy bank balance and brilliant ideas on your side.

Progress comes gradually, as the history of McLaren Mercedes clearly shows. The first two years failed to yield a single race victory, but eight podium

Modesty has always prevented Norbert Haug from demonstrating his talents as a physiotherapist. Here, though, he is pictured prescribing a liquid cure for David Coulthard's aches and pains

The 3-litre Ilmor-built Mercedes engine develops in excess of 850 hp at 18,000 rpm. Excluding the exhaust manifold, it weighs around 90 kilograms

finishes provided a measure of compensation. The turning point came in 1997. Aerodynamics expert and technical director Adrian Newey arrived at McLaren from Williams, West was unveiled as the new title sponsor, and the Arrows were painted silver again. David Coulthard took victory in the first race of the new Formula One season, by the end of which McLaren Mercedes had become a firm fixture at the front of the grid.

The Formula One cars started 1998 with a narrower track and grooved tires, and the Silver Arrows set out in pursuit of victory. Two wins each for Hakkinen and Coulthard ensured that Daimler-Benz – now DaimlerChrysler – was once again making motor sport headlines. The year of the merger ended on a celebratory note, with Mika Hakkinen crowned World Champion – a title he was to retain in 1999.

McLaren Mercedes' return to winning ways was achieved with a combination of state-of-the-art Formula One technology and the individual touches, which all the leading teams hope will give them that extra edge. However, these hard-earned advances can only be secured, if at all, if they are kept confidential.

For this reason data on modern Formula One is extremely hard to come by. Compared with the current Formula One generation, the Grand Prix cars of the past were an open book and could be analyzed down to the last detail.

A look at a McLaren, or any other Formula One racing car for that matter, reveals a unitized construction, like that of a run-of-the-mill road car. The load-bearing centerpiece is known as the monocoque and is constructed from an epoxy resin/carbon fiber composite material. Stronger than comparable sheet steel constructions, this material is also seven times lighter. The monocoque's amazing rigidity gives the Formula One cars the high level of safety demanded by the drivers.

"Carbon fiber composite materials"

have long since replaced high-strength steel in the construction of the long wishbones and diagonal struts. The move towards long control arms to achieve the correct wheel elevation with minimal camber change for which Rudolf Uhlenhaut had striven has continued unabated. The spring travel is, however, shorter now than in his day. After all, today's race tracks are no longer as bumpy as the old Nordschleife in Germany.

Power transmission from the wheels to the central, almost always horizontally mounted shock absorbers is provided by diagonal struts and levers. The stabilizers of

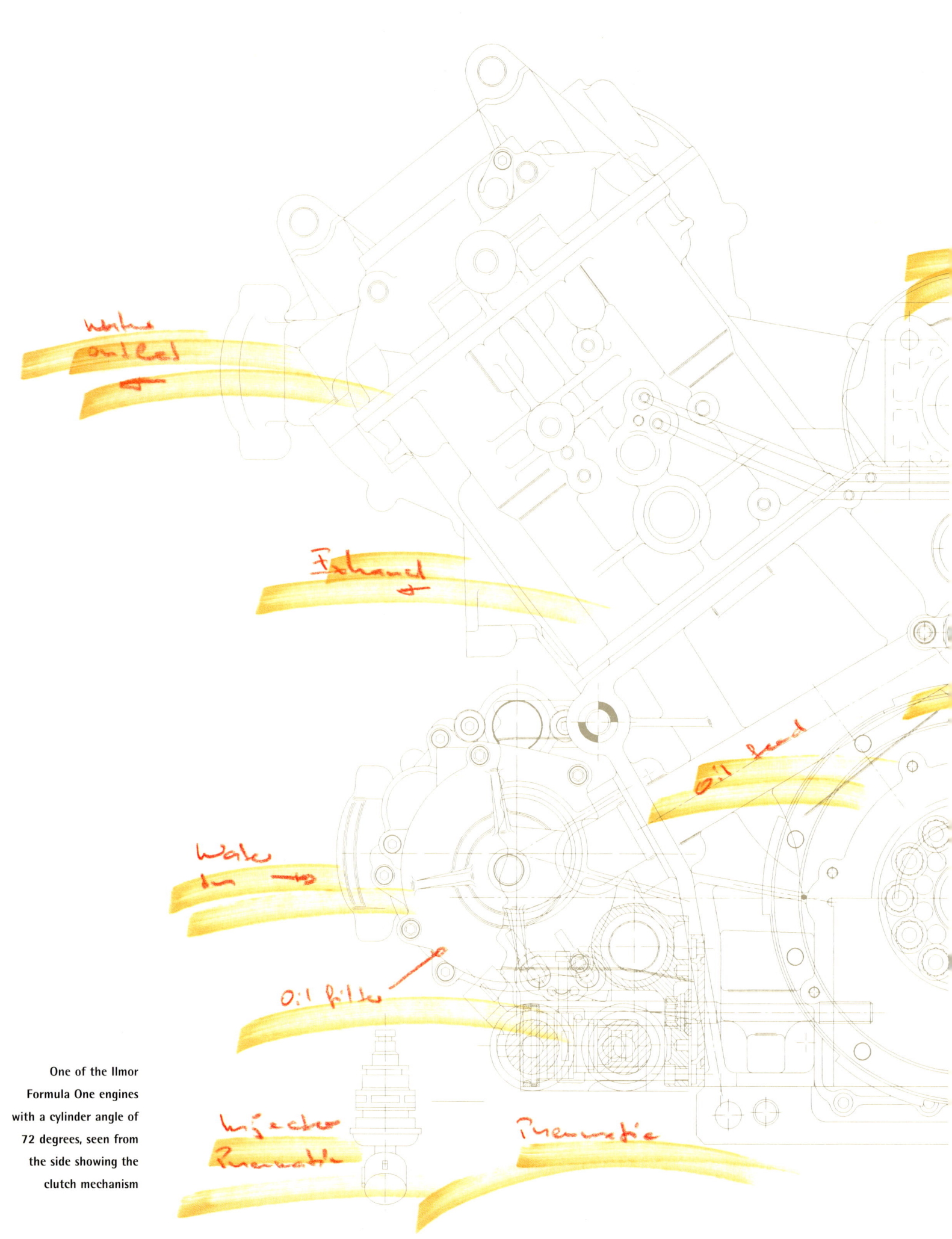

One of the Ilmor Formula One engines with a cylinder angle of 72 degrees, seen from the side showing the clutch mechanism

David Coulthard is a magnate for beautiful women. Even the girls holding his start number seem in a class of their own

Formula One cars are delicate constructions, positioned between the rocker arms of the suspension.

At a time when huge wheels are fitted on sporty production cars as a matter of course, it is astonishing that the Formula One regulations permit only 13-inch wheel rims which look more at home on a supermini. Despite the latest slimming campaign in 1993, tires are still fairly generous in width – rear tires may be up to 15 inches (380 mm) in width. The erstwhile wide-track silhouette of Formula One cars was gradually eroded during the 1990s. Maximum track width was reduced in 1993 from 2150 mm to 2000 mm, and this was cut further to 1800 mm for the 1998 season. The idea was that slimmer cars would make for easier overtaking, but there was an unwanted side effect: the cars got faster. Luckily, their brakes were ready to shoulder the load. Carbon-

The Scottish flag – a white cross on a blue background – has been David Coulthard's trademark ever since a friend painted it on his helmet before his first race

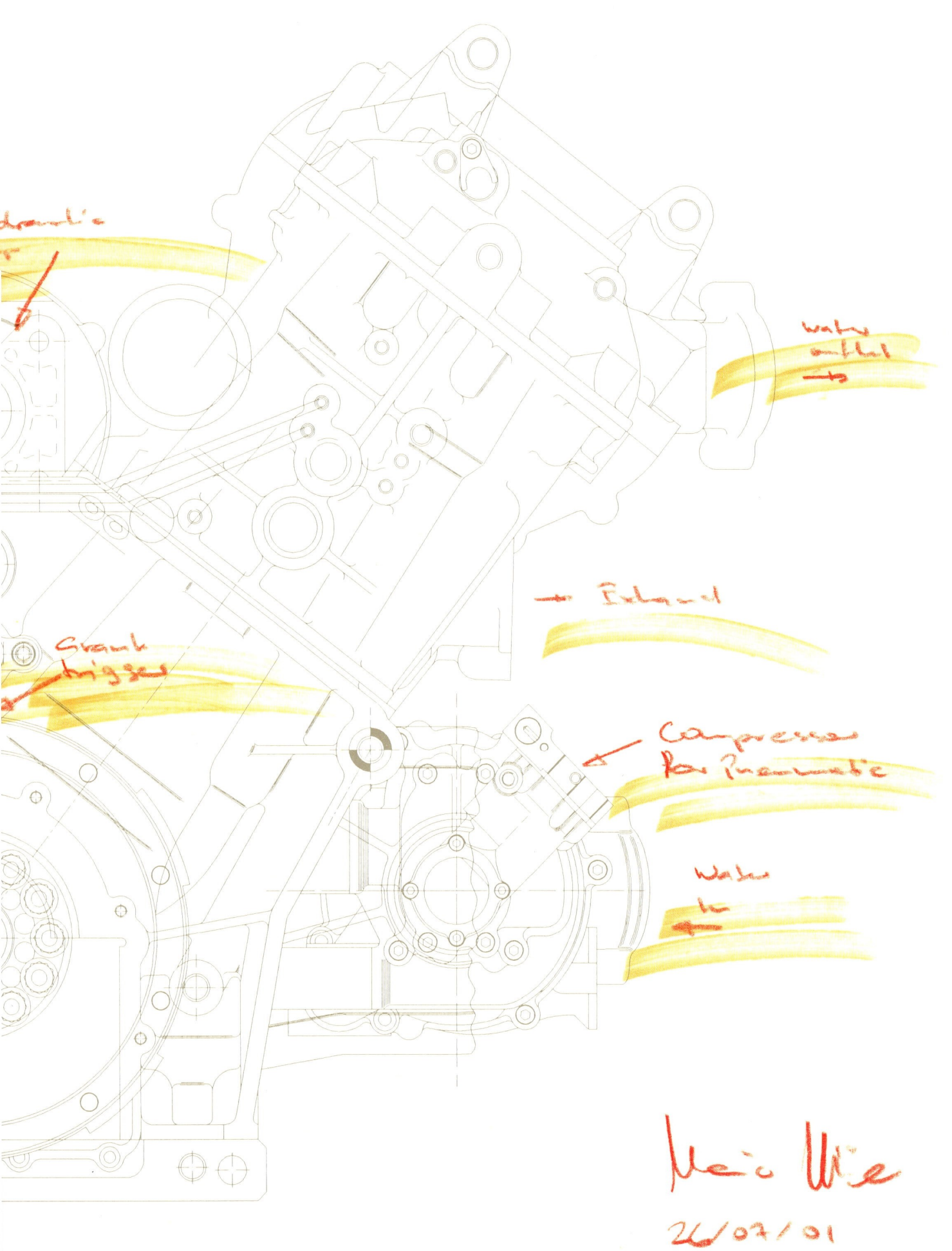

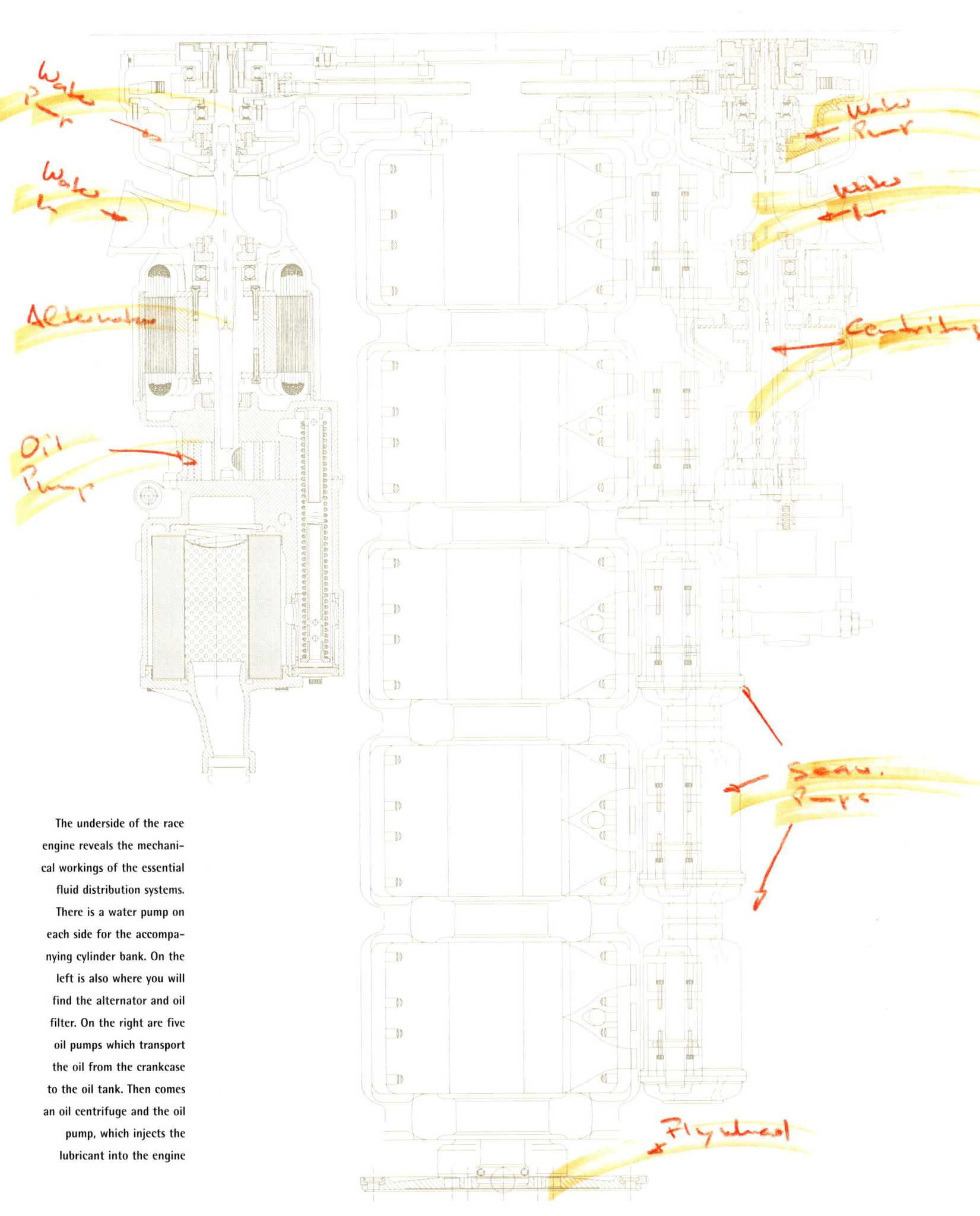

The underside of the race engine reveals the mechanical workings of the essential fluid distribution systems. There is a water pump on each side for the accompanying cylinder bank. On the left is also where you will find the alternator and oil filter. On the right are five oil pumps which transport the oil from the crankcase to the oil tank. Then comes an oil centrifuge and the oil pump, which injects the lubricant into the engine

The water pump, oil centrifuge and oil pumps viewed here from a different perspective

based materials had already proved to be a lighter and thermally superior alternative to the cast iron brake disks a full 20 years previously. Carbon not only cut around four kilograms off the weight of each disk but, more importantly, also reduced the torsional and unsprung masses. Having said that, small torsional masses are actually beneficial when accelerating and braking, and small unsprung masses improve the responses of the suspension, increasing tire grip. The only drawback of these

"lightweight brake disks"

is that they only reach their full friction coefficient at 400 degrees Celsius. Although the basic function of today's Formula One car bodies is still to protect the driver, engine and radiator, in recent times their primary role has been to meet aerodynamic requirements. In contrast to other types of car, the emphasis is not on achieving a low drag coefficient. Quite the contrary, in fact, since the Cd value of a Formula One car would be catastrophic by any normal standards. The designer directs all his efforts towards generating maximum downforce. The idea is that the airstream presses the car as firmly as possible onto the road surface, allowing faster acceleration and braking, and producing extra speed and transverse acceleration through the corners. At high speeds, the aerodynamically generated contact pressure can be as much as 1500 kg, twice the weight of the car. This is dictated by the wing set-up on the car, which is adapted according to the nature of the track and the speeds reached by the cars. One might say, in fact, that fast lap times really are plucked from thin air. The FIA is attempting to keep this somewhat risky game with the laws of physics within limits, and has introduced regulations clipping the cars' wings and regularly limiting alterations to the underbody. But ultimately the engineers will always find a way to create downforce exceeding the cars' weight. In fact, the Formula One cars could in theory drive upside down along the roof of the Monaco tunnel at 200 km/h. In order to generate powerful downforce on the front axle, the nose of Formula One cars sits conspicuously high off the ground. This allows the front wing to do its job more effectively. With all these technical imperatives, the last element in the whole Formula One racing car package to get a look-in is the most adaptable and functional – the driver. Mika Hakkinen, David Coulthard and their rivals in the top category of motor

You have to be pretty quick to get your nose in front in Formula One. A McLaren Mercedes breaks through the 160 km/h barrier in 3.6 seconds

Where else on the planet apart from Hollywood could one hope to find such elegance as in the Formula One paddock

racing all find themselves sitting in their cars as they would

"in the bathtub"

with their legs stretched out in front, feet against the nose-cone. And what's good enough for the driver is good enough for the engine. In order to create the vacuum effect which sucks the car onto the track surface, as much air as possible has to flow and expand under an arched floor panel alongside the engine towards the rear of the car. This means that the engine has to be constructed to fit into the space provided. It has to be slim, which is why most of the V10 units have an acute cylinder angle of between 72 and 80 degrees. The low center of gravity of flatter constructions is not an important factor for Formula One engineers.

The current dominance of V10 engines in Formula One is fundamentally a product of the theory of evolution explaining the survival of the fittest. The 10-cylinder unit is a happy medium between the lighter 8-cylinder, which does not have the same engine speed range, and the 12-cylinder, which has a greater engine speed range but is considerably longer and heavier. Since the regulations are also in favor of preserving the status quo, only 10-cylinder engines are permitted.

With its stake in Ilmor, Mercedes-Benz has the use of one of the most powerful hi-tech Formula One engines on the grid. A relatively new company based in Brixworth, England, Ilmor was founded by the Swiss engineer Mario Illien and his British colleague, the late Paul Morgan. Both had previously worked for race engine specialists Cosworth. Working procedures at Ilmor are rather different from the customary practice of an industry where companies rely on outsourcing and do as little as possible in-house. Ilmor, by contrast, does as much as possible itself, firstly because the work is completed more quickly and with greater precision, and secondly because the world of Formula

Mika Hakkinen also sports a blue and white helmet, the colors of his native Finland

One is riddled with spies. The strength of competition has forced the brilliant engineer Mario Illien to conceive a completely new engine and then rework it every year since 1995. That means he has now reached development stage K – the tenth, in other words. His efforts over this time have yielded the two to four per cent extra power it has required to get back to the top. Time and again, he has also managed to cut the weight of the engine and bring it even further below the 100-kg barrier. Just for the record, the 4-cylinder unit in the Mercedes C 180 is significantly heavier.

Every new development at Mercedes in the 1930s and 1950s was preceded by extensive testing using a single-cylinder test engine, and this is also the case at Ilmor today. This testing is the key to determining optimum combustion chamber geometry and port alignment. However, in contrast to the test engines of the past, Illien's single-cylinder units are built with two balance shafts to prevent them from reaching even a tenth of the output of the full race engine. The Ilmor engineers can accept the consequent loss of friction as, without the mechanical sedative, the free inertia forces of the single-cylinder engine would cause it to explode as soon as it hit 18,000 revolutions.

The Ilmor Formula One engine has a cylinder angle of 72 degrees. The engine housing and cylinder heads are, of course, made of aluminum. The pistons are housed in cast steel bushes. The crankshaft of the V10 has six babbit bearings, and the ten connecting rods run along a similar type of bearing shell in fundamentally the same way as found in a production engine. Oil is supplied by dry sump lubrication. The oil supply is located in a side compartment of the transmission casing. The essential elements of the valve train in the current Formula One engine are actually not as different to that of an ordinary car as they once were. Two overhead camshafts per cylinder bank and four valves per cylinder are no longer the just preserve of such race engines, with even a modest diesel now incorporating such sophisticated technology. Although Illien's use of a rocker arm to activate the valves distances his construction from the somewhat heavier bucket tappet of some of his rivals, comparable engineering does exist in series production cars. One of the fundamental peculiarities of contemporary Formula One engines is their

"lack of valve springs".

The springs used to be positioned concentrically around the valve, where a pneumatic cylinder and a pneumatic piston are now located. The system works at a set gauge pressure which is generated by an air compressor. In short, instead of having conventional titanium coil springs, the valves are air sprung.

This system has the advantage of reducing the moving mass of the valve springs, for although titanium is very light by most standards, air will always be lighter. Furthermore, without the moving mass, a Formula One engine can reach in excess of 18,500 rpm. The single disadvantage of this air-based solution is not a factor in a racing situation, but would be a huge problem in everyday use, since when the engine is stationary, the pressure drops and the valves no longer close properly. This means that the engine can only be started once pressure from a compressed air cylinder is pumped into the system.

The sleeve valves, fitted in place of the throttle

In Monaco, it is the ordinary punter who sits in the grandstand, where a seat for the weekend goes for anything from $ 500 upwards. But anybody who is anybody takes in the race on a giant plasma screen from the comfort of their expensively moored personal yacht

With the onward march of modern technology, the chalk display boards of the 1930s have long since been replaced by digitalised screens. As in the old days, though, they show a good day's work for Mercedes-Benz

caps on the intake side of the cylinder heads, are a special feature of the Ilmor engine. With this departure from the norm, a small gap is created between the throttle element and the intake valves. This allows the car to be tuned perfectly to high engine speeds. In addition, the rotary slide helps the functioning of the length-adjustable velocity stacks, another special feature of the intake stroke of the Ilmor engine. The technique employed by a trombone player to alter the frequency of a note is used in reverse in the Ilmor engine to modulate the resonance in the intake system and improve cylinder filling accordingly. A long tube is used at lower revs, a short one at higher engine speeds.

The modulation of the resonance in the ten intake funnels is controlled by an actuator motor linked to the Motronic control unit. This unit essentially uses the same method as the black box in the latest production cars to ensure that the correct ignition timing is achieved and just the right amount of fuel is injected. Unlike production car engines, though, Formula One power units are not fitted with a catalytic converter. However, both types of engine have an oxygen sensor, which serves as an instrument for monitoring the mixture composition. The output of the 10-cylinder engine was boosted

"from 750 hp to 850 hp"

between 1995 and 2001, requiring an increase in the engine speed range from 14,000 to 18,000 crankshaft revolutions per minute. Some of the credit for the extra power goes to an extremely short stroke, measuring around half the 90-mm bore.

The power transmission system of the McLaren Mercedes has the advantage over a production car of a small but sensitive clutch system. The miracle material carbon makes it possible to channel some 420 Newton meters of torque through a clutch mechanism, whose 180-mm diameter disks have a similar form to those you would otherwise expect to find on an average motorbike. Conventional car clutch mechanisms measure between 200 and 260 mm. The mechanism is activated automatically via hydraulics. Since the 2001 Spanish Grand Prix, launch control has been used to ensure the perfect getaway from the grid. The transmission, which McLaren has manufactured itself, also has an advantage over the sporty 6-speed transmission in Mercedes road cars – a seventh gear. The gear

It was in 1997, their third season, that the new Silver Arrows recaptured their winning form. David Coulthard took the checkered flag at the Australian Grand Prix

change is all fingerwork using two forward-pointing levers in front of the steering wheel. Changing gear with the non-synchronized constant-mesh transmission can be a noisy affair, but as shifting from one gear to the next takes 0.2 seconds the transmission does not really have much time to bare its teeth.

Today's Formula One cars have demonstrated a high level of passive safety when involved in serious accidents, and part of the credit for this must go to the immense strength of the carbon fiber materials and the way they are used in the cars' construction. No less significant in greatly improving the chances of a driver surviving a crash unscathed have been the Formula One regulations designed to maximize safety.

Nowadays, the monocoque structures are subjected to crash tests; cars must be fitted with an extremely robust roll-over bar in case the car flips over; and the cockpit must be designed according to set dimensions and solidity standards in order to guarantee driver safety in the event of a side-on collision with another car. However, some problems remain unresolved, including that of securing wheels more effectively so they no longer turn into dangerous missiles should they come off in a crash.

Model numbers provide sound evidence of the accelerated pace of technical development in Formula One. The seven years of partnership between Mercedes-Benz and McLaren is roughly equivalent to the cycle of a production car model. In Formula One, the cars are updated much more frequently: the 1995 season began with the McLaren MP 4/10; by mid-2001 the McLaren MP 4/16 was lining up on the grid.

The quest for glory and honor still plays a significant role in Formula One and underpins this rush to innovate and improve. But in this game of

"Who Wants to be a Millionaire?"

it is essentially TV ratings which call the tune. The armchair spectator, often enjoying a much better view than the privileged few in the coveted grandstand seats, now holds all the aces in Formula One. For no other sporting event attracts a bigger worldwide audience to their TV sets every fortnight than the 17 Grand Prix races. Indeed, Formula One often wins the battle of the ratings outright on Race Sunday.
It took a glorious summer's evening such as the one that fell on July 1, 2001 for the Circus Maximus of Bernie Ecclestone to lose out to the invincible celluloid Gauls, Asterix and Obelix.

Just getting round the course provides a stiff examination for the drivers in Monaco. Mika Hakkinen rose to the challenge in 1998 and laid the foundations for his World Championship triumph in the process

With its wheelbase of almost three meters and a long, projected, elevated nose section, today's Formula One racecars are a good deal longer than their predecessors. At 4530 mm the McLaren is longer than the Mercedes C-Class

MIKA HAKKINEN

Drivers of the 1990s

When Mika Hakkinen was born on September 28, 1968, Juan Manuel Fangio – his colleague from the second generation of Silver Arrows – was already 57 years old. More than half a century separated the two and in the modern era the road to a World Championship title took a very different route.

Few racing drivers have better demonstrated how times have changed than the young boy Mika from the town of Vantaa near Helsinki. The young Finn first sat behind the wheel of a hired kart at the age of five. But by the time he had completed his first lap, he had joined the relatively short list of drivers of his age to have flipped a racing machine over. The sideways roll seemed not to worry the young Mika unduly, but his parents were not exactly brimming with enthusiasm when their son – before he had even reached school age – insisted that he would one day grow up to become a racing driver.

The purchase of even his first kart went well beyond the financial means of Mika's parents, both of whom worked – his father Harri was a radio operator with a shipping radio station in the Gulf of Finland, his mother Aila a part-time secretary. In order to finance the kart Mika so longed for, Harri began moonlighting as a taxi driver, putting money to one side until he had saved the 1000 Finnish marks he needed to buy a secondhand machine from a certain Henry Toivonen. (Toivonen was later to become World Rally Driving Champion and tragically lost his life during the 1986 Corsican Rally.)

The price of the kart – roughly equivalent to $140 – was a considerable sum for Mika's parents at the time. But when their son decided to commit himself to the pursuit of his chosen career, Harri Hakkinen was left no choice but to continue

"driving taxis"

for another six years – alongside his work as a radio operator – in order to finance Mika's hobby. In the early years, the kart racing was purely for fun. Competitions in Finland were open only to boys and girls over the age of twelve. So Mika was obliged to wait until 1980.

For anybody hoping to race seriously in the eighties, professional equipment was an absolute must. So Harri Hakkinen turned to Pekka Pirkola, who built kart chassis and imported kart parts. Pirkola sold him a "Finnkart" for his son, and seeing as technical support came as part of the after-sales service, Harri was now no longer obliged to spend time working on his son's karts. Maintenance became the job of Pekka Pirkola.

The 1980 season provided no heroic deeds worth recording here. But in 1981 Mika Hakkinen won his first Finnish championship title and in so doing caught the attention of the "Blue Rose" team. This team took him on in 1982, and between 1983 and 1986 Mika Hakkinen was showered with titles, taking four in a row. It was during this period that Mika befriended his kart sport opponent Mika Sohlberg, son of Kari Sohlberg, President of the Finnish Motor Sports Association and a wealthy motor racing sponsor. Moreover, at the 1984 Junior World Championships in Laval in France Hakkinen had his first encounter with Michael Schumacher. But this early contest between the two ended at the semi-final stage when Mika developed problems with his carburetor.

By the time Hakkinen finally reached his eighteenth birthday in September 1986, he had already decided to give up karting, with the aim of moving on to greater things. What he really wanted to drive was a proper racing car.

As entrance tickets into the world of motor racing go, a Formula Ford 1600 was just about affordable. With the financial help of a few willing sponsors – one of whom was Kari Sohlberg – Mika got hold of a good one-year-old Reynard from his countryman JJ Lehto. His friend Mika Sohlberg took on the job of manager and with two full-time mechanics to support them

"Team Mika & Mika"

enjoyed a fantastic season. By the end of 1987 Hakkinen had taken the Finnish, Swedish and Nordic championship titles in Formula Ford 1600.

In October 1987 the sponsors Marlboro issued invitations requesting the pleasure of the season's best junior drivers at a "talent competition" on the race circuit at Donington Castle. For the successful few there was the reward of a year-long scholarship in one of the intermediate racing categories. During the trials Jean Alesi and Volker Weidler qualified for Formula 3000, Eddie Irvine and JJ Lehto made it into Formula 3, and Mika Hakkinen and Allan McNish would be proving their talents in the 1988 season in a new formula. This was to comprise the Opel-Lotus Challenge, a series of ten races for the European Championship, together with the ten-race Vauxhall-Lotus Challenge for the British Championships.

This switch to the international scene meant that Mika had to leave his Finnish family and friends behind, move to England and learn

Left-hand page: Mika Hakkinen has been driving the McLaren-Mercedes in traditional silver since West joined as sponsors

Much has been written of Mika Hakkinen's ability to shut out the stress of Formula One racing. This picture by photographer Wolfgang Wilhelm would seem to refute the written theories, however

Double delight: Mika Hakkinen wins at the 1998 Japanese Grand Prix and is crowned World Champion for the second time

to speak English – not something that came easily. Both Hakkinen and McNish were sponsored by Marlboro to drive for the

"Dragon team"

and in the 1988 season they took a firm control of the competition and shared the spoils between them – the Scot McNish winning the UK title and Hakkinen becoming European Champion.

In 1989 Mika Hakkinen moved up to Formula 3 with Dragon, but his choice of car – a Reynard with a Toyota engine – turned out to be ill-judged. At the end of the season, by which time the championship had long since been decided, Mika switched to driving a Ralt-Mugen Honda belonging to the West Surrey team. A convincing victory at Brands Hatch was enough to restore Hakkinen's self-confidence. He spent the 1990 season driving for West Surrey alongside Christian Fittipaldi and won the British Championships by a country mile.

Preparations for his move up to Formula One began in 1990. Mika's manager Keke Rosberg was already making the necessary contacts, and both Lotus and Benetton had shown interest in the Flying Finn. During preliminary testing at Silverstone, Mika found he could push the Benetton to a good speed straight off. But it was Lotus who won the poker game to secure the contract.

At this stage in its history, the traditional English brand was now no longer the force it once was. As a result, Mika Hakkinen's entry into Formula One in 1991 was not the glittering success he had hoped for.

The Lotus' chronically frail Judd engine failed the Finn on seven occasions and left him trailing with just two points in a lowly fifteenth position in the championship. The 1992 season ended a little more successfully. Driving the Lotus Ford, Mika Hakkinen finished eighth with eleven championship points. And with that, Mika's prospects also improved. Not only was Peter Collins keen to keep Mika with Lotus, now Frank Williams had Hakkinen on his list and Ron Dennis was looking for a third driver for McLaren. And this third driver would have to do what Mika had never particularly enjoyed doing: test driving – and lots of it!

Ayrton Senna and Michael Andretti had already secured the contracts to race, so all Mika could expect was to keep the reserve bench warm. Keke Rosberg advised against taking the risk with McLaren at this stage, because as a test driver he would be out of the Formula One scene for a whole year. Hakkinen decided to sign nonetheless.

"Mika bided his time"

whilst continuing with the test driving. His big moment came after thirteen races, when Michael Andretti decided to quit Formula One. And so on September 26, 1993, Mika lined up alongside teammate Ayrton Senna at the start of the Portuguese Grand Prix at Estoril.

In 1994, McLaren's year with Peugeot engines, doubts began to creep into Hakkinen's mind that he had really landed himself a place in one of the top teams. Out of the first nine races, he finished only two. But towards the end of the season he was able to prove his driving ability with one second and five third places.

For McLaren, though, the early years using the Mercedes-Benz engines designed at Ilmor were a barren period. In 1995 Mika succeeded only in achieving a negative record of nine retirements. Worse still, a life endangering crash during the last race of the season at the Australian Grand Prix in Adelaide put the seal on a tragic season.

Mika Hakkinen had to wait almost two years for his fortunes to change. Finally, on October 26, 1997, he won his first Formula One race – the European Grand Prix in Jerez, Spain – driving the McLaren-Mercedes. One year and eight wins later he was crowned World Champion for the first time and for a second time twelve months after that.

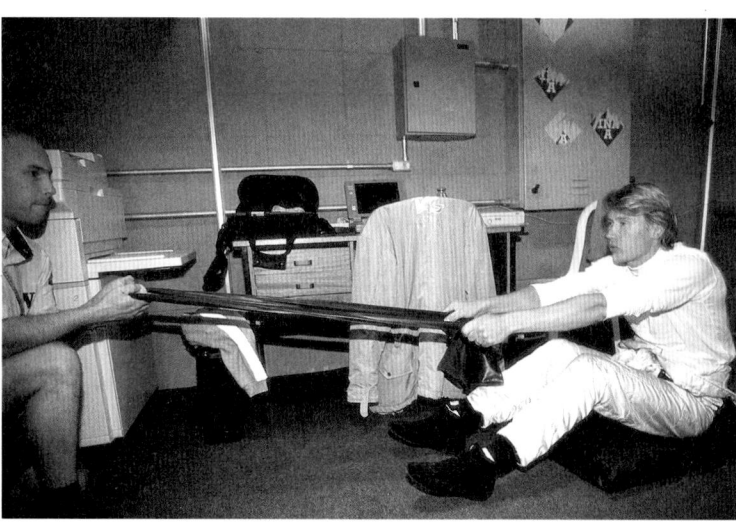

Although Mika appears to be deriving little enjoyment from this fitness routine, it is vital for top Formula One drivers to train regularly these days

DAVID COULTHARD

The Scot David Coulthard sees it as his role to continue the glorious tradition of Scottish World Champions in Formula One. His idol Jim Clark won the title in 1963 and 1965, Jackie Stewart achieved the same feat in 1969, 1971 and 1973.

The young man from Kirkcudbrightshire, known to his friends simply as DC, is the smiling member of the team. If things had not worked out so well with racing, he would have happily settled for the life of a musician

The more detailed maps of Great Britain show Twynholm as a speck near Dumfries in the county of Kirkcudbrightshire. This tiny village in southwest Scotland has fewer than three hundred inhabitants – among them, the Coulthard family. David's father Duncan has successfully turned the family's small haulage business into an international concern – though as a good Scot, Duncan plays down his wealth, arguing that the company airplane he uses for quick hops to business appointments is a vital tool rather than a symbol of affluence. As a young man, he would have preferred to have enjoyed the sensation of speed in other ways. But sadly for him his career in kart sport never really took off and in the end he attached greater importance to developing the business.

But it was already clear that a man such as Duncan Coulthard would prove to be

"the ideal father"

to a son whose sole ambition in life

was to become a racing driver. Duncan was given the chance to hand his own boyhood dream down a generation when his wife Joyce provided him with a daughter Linsey and two sons – one named Duncan like his father, and destined to take over the family business, and a second, David, born on March 27, 1971.

From the very beginning, Duncan senior was only too happy to indulge his boys' passion for motorized toys. They were given small motorbikes and by the age of eight David was driving a kart around a makeshift circuit normally reserved as a parking lot for his dad's trucks. It was not long, however, before a proper kart track opened up near Twynholm.

This was all the encouragement Duncan Coulthard needed to enter the world of motor sport as a team manager. The first driver for

"Coulthards Racing"

was Brian Smith. And as soon as he reached the age of twelve, young David entered his first kart races – much to the delight of his parents.

The racing debut of Coulthard Junior – known now to his friends simply as DC – took place on the Kirkcudbrightshire circuit in 1982, and although he managed to avoid a repeat of that spectacular feat performed by the five-year-old Mika Hakkinen, the result was less than memorable. But before the season was much older he was to make rapid progress towards the podium places. The climax to the season was a duel for the Scottish Junior Championships.

His opponent was three years his senior, had three years' more experience and was already on the way up. His name was Allan McNish. Faced with such experience, the young Coulthard had little realistic prospect of winning. But it was not his destiny to be runner-up for long. McNish switched to Formula Ford 1600 and from 1983 onwards DC took the number one spot in the Scottish Junior Championships. Having taken three junior titles he moved up to senior level, and here, too, he twice became champion.

The next rung of the ladder – a move into a proper racing car – naturally required a helping hand from his father Duncan. He arranged a meeting of three Davids in the fall of 1988 on the race track at Knoxhill north of Edinburgh – David Coulthard was to meet David Leslie senior and his son, also called David Leslie. The Leslies had a small racing team with a Formula Ford 1600 and were prepared to let any qualified driver race providing they had the necessary cash.

So there at Knoxhill, DC took the wheel of the Leslie's Van Diemen and obviously impressed with his speed. He finished a successful 1989 season exactly as planned – by the fall he was the Formula Ford 1600

"British Champion."

And for this achievement he was to get an additional pat on the back of recognition. The "Young Driver of the Year" award for 1989 – presented jointly by World Champions McLaren and Autosport magazine – went to David Coulthard. And the prize included a rather special prize – the Young Driver of the Year was given the chance to complete a few laps in a McLaren Formula One car.

Whilst in 1990 McLaren was sponsoring Allan McNish, David Coulthard joined Paul Stewart Racing, a team which – although based in Milton Keynes in England – was Scottish through and through. The company had been founded by Jackie Stewart for his son Paul, his parents evidently happier to see their offspring go into team management rather than racing. It goes without saying, of course, that once again Coulthard's father Duncan was required to dip into his pockets.

In the 1990 season PSR took part in the Vauxhall-Lotus Challenge races, in which Mika Hakkinen had also been involved two years earlier. Although David Coulthard could not match the Finn's brilliant season, he still finished with a fourth place in the British Championships and the Stewarts were satisfied with DC's performance. He was offered a contract for the following season to race in Formula 3.

In 1991 things got better and better for David. He was consistently there or thereabouts at the front of races and the championship soon developed into a contest between David Coulthard and Rubens Barrichello. Eventually, having defeated the Brazilian on five occasions, the Scot lost the title owing to a shunt in the final race. He finished the championships runner-up.

The 1992 season brought further promotion for DC – PSR moved up to Formula 3000. Paul Stewart was now in his early twenties and still without any significant racing experience, but he could no longer resist the temptation to drive one of the powerful cars himself. For DC this meant the delicate

diplomatic task of racing against the team manager's son. But since no member of the team reached the podium that season, relationships remained relaxed. David could console himself with the fact that his ninth place in the Formula 3000 European Championships was still well ahead of Allan McNish and Paul Stewart. And in any case, DC could be quietly pleased with the fruits of what the records showed to be a rather meager season, for he had got a foot in the door of Formula One – as a test driver with Benetton.

Coulthard's time with Stewart Racing came to an end with the close of the 1992 season. His father Duncan was forced to make cuts in the family's racing budget, so a contract with the financially less demanding Team Pacific enabled DC to remain in Formula 3000. In 1993 he found himself climbing the podium more regularly, and at the end of the Sicilian race in Enna he even took the top step. He finished the European Championships in third place. David's greatest success during that year, however, came from an entirely different quarter. Together with David Brabham and John Nielson he won the GT category at the 24-hour Le Mans race in a Jaguar XK220. He also continued Formula One test driving – but by this time he had joined the top class Williams-Renault team.

In May 1994 David Coulthard was forced to live through the same tragedy as many test drivers before him. At the San Marino Grand Prix in Imola the circuit claimed the lives of both Roland Ratzenberger and DC's Williams teammate Ayrton Senna. After a gap of one race, David found himself taking Senna's place at the start of the Barcelona Grand Prix. But DC had to share his place in the team alongside Damon Hill with Nigel Mansell, who was scheduled to drive four races for Williams in addition to his latest activities in the American CART series.

The situation was to change in 1995, however. DC succeeded in convincing Frank Williams of his driving qualities and after a brief period of flirting with McLaren at the poker phase of contract negotiations, he was finally offered a proper driver's contract by Williams for the 1995 season. In his first full season in Formula One he underlined the confidence shown in him with a win at Estoril, five pole positions and seven podium places.

When David Coulthard joined McLaren-Mercedes in 1996, one year after Mika Hakkinen, the team was still in its development phase. As runner-up in Monaco, third-placed at the Nürburgring and an overall seventh in the championships, DC's balance sheet was certainly not as positive as it had been the previous year.

But the upturn came in 1997. Now appearing as West McLaren-Mercedes, the racing cars once again sported a hint of traditional silver. And that seemed to do the trick. The opening race of the season in Adelaide saw David Coulthard cross the finish first. He went on to win a second time in Monza and was runner-up in the Austrian and European Grand Prix. His 36 points at the end of the season left him well ahead of teammate Hakkinen, whose best years were just about to start.

David Coulthard stays fit by taking his mountain-bike into the hills behind his adopted home in Monaco. And it is here on the Côte d'Azur that the Scot hopes to settle when his career as a racing driver is over

Left-hand page: David also manages to find perfect balance on two wheels in the McLaren-Mercedes

A new trophy in the background is the cause for celebration: David Coulthard with Jürgen Hubbert and Norbert Haug

UNSUNG HEROES

Patrolling the pits

The knowledge that races are not won on the track alone but also in the pits dates back long before the Silver Arrows. No driver could ever have completed that first 500-mile race at Indianapolis in 1911 without some assistance from the pits for refueling and mechanical matters. Equally, the successful premiere of 24-hour race at Le Mans in 1923 was largely thanks to the willing squad of helpers behind every team of drivers, who ensured that the cars kept going and going.

But the mechanics whose job it is to perform a refueling or wheel change at lightning speed have always been the sport's unsung heroes. What they take home at the end of a race bears no comparison with the salary of the drivers they serve. Nor is there a laurel wreath or trophy to reward a job well done.

Even the language has been unkind to their workplace. Whether one takes the Anglo-American term "pits" or its German equivalent "Boxen", the image remains the same – these frenzied workers have been forever destined to work in cramped and confined spaces. The term originally served to describe what it actually was –

"a hole in the ground"

or, at best, a trench. Admittedly by 1934 things had moved on a little from the Stone Age conditions of the earliest races, but one can hardly imagine that that long night before the Eifel race, during which the white Mercedes-Benz cars were transformed into the now legendary Silver Arrows using only paintscrapers, sandpaper and emery cloth, was spent in any great comfort. The drivers' enclosure provided rooms barely bigger than a garage, whilst up at track level Alfred Neubauer and his team worked in even pokier dens. The ambient temperature – either red-hot or icy cold – was left to the vagaries of the Eifel climate.

The regulations which controlled the number of people permitted to work in the pits were certainly no job creation scheme designed to reduce unemployment. Only three people were allowed in contact with the car. One of these would heave the car up on its

In the 1930s a maximum of three mechanics were allowed at pit stops during the race. In this picture taken during practice there were a few more hands than usual to help with the rather risky refueling procedure. Nowadays a team of twenty-two are ready to spring into action for that eight-second pit stop

The tires were noticeably narrower in the 1930s, although supplies were plentiful. But the mechanics still had the tricky task of centering the wire-spoked wheels

axles using a wheel jack, a principle which survives today in modern Formula One. It was then the job of the other two to loosen the so-called Rudge nuts on the wheels using a copper hammer – a task which often brought success only after several attempts or, occasionally, not at all. Then it was up to the man on each side of the car to remove the old wheel and single-handedly replace it with the new one. Finally it was back to work with the hammer to tighten the nuts. The best time recorded for such wheel changes was about 26 seconds. But the practices developed for rapid refueling were, if anything, even more archaic.

Hundreds of liters of the highly toxic fuel mix were transferred to the cars

"using milk churns and funnels."

Indeed one of the safety features of the early Silver Arrows was the location of the rear tank well away from the hot exhaust manifolds.

The fact that such operations as these were occasionally prone to go wrong was something which Manfred von Brauchitsch learned to his cost in the 1938 Grand Prix at the Nürburgring. Escaping fuel caught fire and Alfred Neubauer had to pull the driver out of the cockpit to escape the sea of flames.

In his role as racing team manager at Mercedes-Benz, Neubauer had redefined the strategic work carried out trackside even before the era of the Silver Arrows had begun. Years earlier, he had devised a system to give drivers the information they needed by chalking it up on boards. And the business of timing he had down to a fine art – there is hardly a picture of Neubauer which does not show him with stopwatch in hand.

But in those days, where timekeeping was concerned, it was every man for himself. Team managers kept several clocks running and the drivers would even give their wives or girlfriends a chronometer to hold – a sort of mechanical medicine to bring relief to their anxieties. After a while, many of them became part of the regular team, helping to record accurate lap times for the drivers.

Twenty years later, when the second generation of Silver Arrows was preparing to challenge for a World Championship title, little had changed in the pits at all. Alfred Neubauer had long since returned to his full fighting weight and was still fingering the same old stopwatch. There were a few new drivers calling in for service – and, as a consequence, one or two new faces among the ladies. Some were even roped in to help with the timekeeping. The fact that in 1942 a certain Konrad Zuse had built his first computer, the Z2, had absolutely no impact on the way things were done in Formula One.

Nowadays the number of tires permitted is restricted: three sets per car in practice and a maximum of seven sets – including intermediates and wet weather tires – for use in qualifying and the race itself

In Fangio's day the mechanics in their overalls still had time to stretch out and enjoy a relaxing cigarette break under a parasol

The great-grandmother of all laptops would in any case have been far too space-hungry for the pits.

Apart from timekeeping and the need to up-date the race order boards, life in the pits during Grand Prix races in the 1950s had generally become a lot less stressful. Distances had been cut, and the smaller engines not only consumed less fuel, they were also less punishing on the more hard-wearing tires.

"Refueling became unnecessary"

and tire changes occurred only as the result of an unexpected problem. Occasionally races were still won strategically from the pits, but in the case of Formula One races, at least, the mechanics were no longer the unsung heroes who could make or break it for a driver as had previously been the case. Anyone requiring technical assistance had generally already blown his chance.

Few fundamental changes took place then over the next forty years. Although the engines became more powerful, the races became shorter, so Formula One could continue to do without planned pit stops.

This was not to change until 1994. Then came a call from Bernie Ecclestone for a return to the good old days. In a move to increase excitement and improve the spectacle for television, he brought about a renaissance of the pit stop by decreeing that in future each car must make at least one refueling stop in each race.

The refueling stop made compulsory by the change to the regulations also led promptly to a reconsideration of tire issues. The thinking was simple: if a driver was already obliged to make a lengthy stop to refuel anyway, then why not equip the car with a new set of tires to improve its performance for the second half of the race. Furthermore, tire companies saw this as a golden opportunity to improve tire grip at the expense of durability.

The pit stop has now become a permanent feature of the slick and shrewdly directed Grand Prix mini-drama. Over the years, the heroic four-hour races

have gradually been tailored to a feature film length of two hours to pander to television audiences.

Close-up shots of the action in the pits are what the majority of small-screen viewers most want to see. Here the tension is at its highest, for here the entrenched battles for position are temporarily broken off – this is where races can be won and lost.

The fact that from 1994 races lasted a few minutes longer than previously was not entirely the result of the obligatory pit stop. Lap times show that alterations to technical regulations had also slowed the cars down.

With the return of the compulsory pit stop, the 1994 German Grand Prix offered a first – and hopefully last – reminder that high-speed refueling can mean "playing with fire". For Dutchman Jos Verstappen, the refueling stop in the Benetton pits ended in a sea of flames, from which he managed to escape with

Today the fastest customer service team in the world – dressed in flameproof suits and integral helmets – waits nervously to make its brief appearance in the public eye. The floor of the air-conditioned McLaren pits always has a fresh coat of paint

In the pits | 149

just superficial burns thanks to the skill and experience of the firemen on hand.

In 1995 Mercedes-Benz entered the Grand Prix arena for a third time, now partnering McLaren. The sport's dimensions had changed radically since the 1950s. The number of cars per team may have been limited to two, but the effort and expense required to contend for the World Championship title had grown disproportionately large. Twenty-five metric tons of equipment is packed for shipment to each race, including two race cars and one reserve car, as well as the essential parts for ten or twelve engines and four transmission systems. And since the re-introduction of tire changes during the race, racing partner Bridgestone was obliged to supply 40 tires per car for each race.

Pit stops nowadays decide the outcome of races more than at any time in the past. Success is the product of a complex mathematical exercise. On the one hand, the volume of fuel has to be calculated, since the weight of on-board fuel determines lap times – less fuel equals higher speeds. The engineers are able to calculate with a great degree of accuracy at what point an optimum speed-weight ratio is reached. One of the pre-race strategic questions asked of the tactical wizards is usually, therefore, at what point in the race should the car be light and fast and have less fuel on-board? The McLaren-Mercedes team can rely on the very economical Ilmor engine and therefore often opt for a late refueling stop. This allows Hakkinen or Coulthard to continue clocking up the laps in lightweight cars, unimpeded by opponents who have been forced into the pits early.

Of considerably greater complexity is the search for the perfect choice of tire – even when dry weather seems to make the decision an easy one – because teams must select the correct rubber composite on the Saturday before qualifying for their grid positions, and stick with their choice through to the race on Sunday. Moreover, the hardness of the tires does not just determine grip and best lap times, it also affects wear and durability. So the aim is to achieve success by adopting a compromise solution, ensuring that the

"refueling and tire change"

occur at a point in the race when there is still just enough left in the tank and on the tires.

Whereas Alfred Neubauer had to take charge of his three mechanics himself, Ron Dennis as head of McLaren-Mercedes can rely on the fact that behind

Then as now, racing cars had no built-in starter and relied on the principle of a separate starter unit. Nowadays they look a little less cumbersome, however, and are inserted at the rear

Diagnostic tests on electronic systems are carried out nowadays with the aid of sophisticated computer software. And for mechanical problems, the engineers can peer deep inside their patient using a doctor's endoscope

him in the pit lane team manager Dave Ryan is busy coordinating a much larger squad. Clearly the F.I.A. is keen to do its bit to create employment opportunities, since it has never imposed an upper limit on the number of people permitted to help with a pit stop.

McLaren-Mercedes has a team of no fewer than 22 around the car:

- Twelve mechanics are required for the wheel changes alone – three per wheel is now as many as was once permitted for the entire pit stop.
- Two strapping lads literally support the work of the wheel-changers by operating the front and rear car jacks.
- Four are responsible for the re-fueling process. Together they must ensure that fuel is delivered safely and at the precise rate of twelve liters per second. One member of the team handles the fuel hose, a second secures it, a third wipes up any spillage and the fourth co-ordinates the whole procedure.
- A fireman stands at the ready with a fire extinguisher.
- A further safety mechanic checks that the jacked-up car remains stable.
- An emergency helper is also standing by with a starter unit in case the driver stalls the engine.
- And one member of the team takes the role of lollipop man, whose job is to stand in front of the car holding a large disc to signal to a driver when to apply the brakes and when to accelerate away.

In total there are therefore almost ten times as many people working on the cars in the pits as was previously permitted. Tire changes are the sole responsibility of the twelve on the wheels; and the two jack operators can do their job eleven times faster than the trio six decades before them. In the 1930s it took 42 seconds to change the four tires; today, using a pneumatic air gun, the tire-change takes just 3.8 seconds – less time than you or I would take to check a single tire pressure.

Quick pit stop times have always been the fruit of hard training. Alfred Neubauer would rehearse the procedures for tire changes and refueling with his mechanics over and over again. But time for training was much more limited in the early days of racing

Once upon a time the humble magnifying glass – seen here helping experts from Bosch's racing department to diagnose spark plug trouble – was a most vital scientific aid

Until well into the 1950s, each team was responsible for keeping its own lap times. A position somewhere near the start/finish line was satisfactory – as can be seen from the two well-dressed time-keepers in Donington 1937 pictured here

than it is today, since pit mechanics had to spend a much larger proportion of their time between races working fixed hours in the racing department.

Work in the pits has now become almost a full-time job, and as a result preparations begin in earnest in February each year. Pit stops for the season ahead are rehearsed at a disused airfield close to company headquarters in Woking where trials are carried out using different combinations of personnel in the individual roles. The degree of perfection to which they carry out their tasks are evaluated not just by means of the stopwatch, but also using video recordings to enable processes to be analyzed in detail.

"That's how we arrive at the perfectly choreographed pit stop", explains Dave Ryan. "We find out which mechanic fits best into each position – in other words, we get the best job done in the shortest possible time."

Intensive training carries on throughout the season. Each Thursday before a race the McLaren-Mercedes pit team goes through the so-called

"wet test".

Stepping out of the pits in their full regalia, the 22-man team is required to practice tire changes and refueling with defined quantities of gasoline. As this theatrical cameo is rehearsed up to 30 times, the team's flameproof suits have a tendency to become rather moist on the inside. And on the morning of race-day, Sunday, there is not just a "warm-up" for drivers and cars. The workers in the pits are required to get themselves back up to running temperature with a dry test. This time refueling is practiced without gasoline.

But far more has changed in and around the Formula One pits than just the number of men working there. As has been the case with race circuits generally, safety has increased enormously over the years. Although in Alfred Neubauer's day the pit area was usually a little wider in order to speed up service, there was no such thing as a pit lane and no attempt was made to establish a clear separation of racing and refueling – let alone impose a speed limit on approach.

Even though the mechanics' working environment is now no longer anywhere near the circuit

Even in the 1950s, Formula One teams were simply left standing out in the paddock when it rained

Although disinfectant is not yet compulsory, the McLaren pits are nowadays as clean as an operating theater. And unlike the blue dungarees of yesteryear, each team member wears a fresh set of team clothes every day

itself, safety regulations are much more stringent than they ever used to be. Anyone going about their business in the pits today is obliged to wear protection of significantly better quality than was available to World Champion Fangio, for example, or to any number of subsequent title holders. Suits, gloves and underclothing have to be made of regulation flameproof materials and a test standard

"integral crash helmet"

is compulsory. Compared with the old milk churn and funnel of the 1930s, the refueling system used today is just about as safe as it gets. A valve in the filling hose and a second one in the tank ensure that fuel can only be pumped as long as there is a perfect connection. It is impossible for large quantities of fuel to spill out during filling, and any traces of combustible fumes escaping during the re-fueling process are sucked away via a duct in the fuel hose.

The highly toxic cocktails which were once used to power racing cars have long since been banned. Nevertheless, the fuel used in Formula One is not quite the same as that sold to motorists at the filling station – with an octane rating of 102 it is just a shade higher than standard super unleaded.

Even though the team of workers in the pits has increased dramatically in size over the years, one job – and a very important one at that – has been rationalized as a result of technical progress. The ladies and gentlemen who looked after the stopwatches now no longer sit in the pits. Since official timekeeping data can now be sent to a number of different monitors directly via a complex and extensive computer network, the whole team can be kept abreast of lap times down to the last thousandth of a second.

However, there are now plenty of others in the pits whose job it is to gather and analyze all sorts of other data. Thanks to telemetry it is nowadays possible to transmit encrypted information relating to the car's driving dynamics and engine performance from the racing car back to the data analysts and software engineers – indispensable players in the modern racing team. Each season they process a flood of data from races and test runs which add up to near enough 100 gigabytes.

If they were to save to disk everything they recorded in the course of a year, they would end up with a small but costly collection of 30 CD-ROMs, costing more than five million marks each.

The barn-like conditions in which the team mechanics used to work on the Mercedes W25 are a little reminiscent of a certain stable in Bethlehem

GRAND PRIX DRIVERS PAST AND PRESENT

1934-1939

RUDOLF CARACCIOLA (D/CH)
*January 30, 1901
†September 28, 1959

Career as racing driver from 1920 to 1952.
Joined Mercedes as works driver in 1923, three times European Champion and 17 wins in Mercedes Silver Arrows, a total of over 100 wins in races and rallies

MANFRED VON BRAUCHITSCH (D)
*August 15, 1905

Career as racing driver from 1928 to 1939.
Eleven wins as an independent driver in a Mercedes-Benz. Works driver from 1934. Won first Silver Arrows race and two Grands Prix

HERMANN LANG (D)
*April 9, 1909
†October 19, 1987

Career as racing driver on two and four wheels from 1928 to 1954. Started out as mechanic in the Mercedes-Benz racing department, then joined the team as a junior driver in 1935. Became European Champion and European Hillclimb Champion in 1939

JOHN RICHARD BEATTIE SEAMAN (GB)
*February 4, 1913
†June 25, 1939

Career as racing driver from 1931 to 1939.
Works driver for Mercedes-Benz from 1937 to 1939, won 1938 German Grand Prix, fatally injured during 1939 Belgian Grand Prix

LUIGI FAGIOLI (I)
*January 9, 1898
†June 20, 1952

Career as racing driver from 1925 to 1952.
In 1928 had eleven wins in sports car races, Grand Prix teams: 1931 Maserati, 1933 Alfa-Romeo squad of Scuderia Ferrari, 1934 Mercedes-Benz, 1937 Auto Union

LOUIS CHIRON (F)
*August 3, 1899
†June 22, 1979

Career as racing driver from 1924 to 1955.
A knight of the French Legion of Honor, he found great success with his Bugatti, winning 27 Grands Prix in total. In 1932 he co-founded the Scuderia C.C. with Caracciola, had no success in the 1936 season for Mercedes, won the 1954 Monte Carlo rally and became Commissaire Général of A.C. Monaco

HANNS GEIER (D)
*February 25, 1902
†November 7, 1986

Career as racing driver from 1933 to 1939.
Showed a great deal of promise as a junior driver in the 1934/35 seasons in the Mercedes Grand Prix car. Following a serious accident in Bern, he went on to become a successful endurance driver, working as assistant to Alfred Neubauer

HANS HUGO HARTMANN (D)
*February 8, 1916
†February 1991

Career as racing driver from 1935 to 1954.
Drove for Mercedes in the 1939 season as a junior team member in the Swiss Grand Prix and Eifelrennen. Almost won the 1953 Carrera Panamericana in the 1.5 l class, but was disqualified for finishing the last stage 7 seconds outside the permitted time

HEINZ BRENDEL (D)
*January 16, 1915

Career as racing driver from 1932 to 1939.
After successes in sports car racing with Fiat and endurance drives with Mercedes, he joined the squad of junior drivers in 1936. He replaced Dick Seaman in the 1939 German Grand Prix, but crashed during testing and escaped from his car with serious burns

GOFFREDO ZEHENDER (I)
*February 27, 1901
†January 7, 1958

Career as racing driver from 1924 to 1939.
He was a junior and reserve driver for the Mercedes-Benz racing team from 1936 to 1937. His best result was a fifth place at the Monaco Grand Prix of 1937

CHRISTIAN KAUTZ (CH)
*November 23, 1913
†July 4, 1948

Career as racing driver from 1934 to 1948.
The Swiss was a reserve driver for the Mercedes team in the 1937 season and finished the Belgian Grand Prix in fourth place. In 1948 he suffered a fatal accident at the Swiss Grand Prix

ERNST HENNE (D)
*February 22, 1904

Career as racing driver from 1924 to 1937.
After great success racing motorbikes, Munich-born Henne started as a junior driver for Mercedes in 1934. In 1937, riding a BMW, he set a motorbike world record of 279.6 km/h which stood until 1951

WALTER BÄUMER (D)
*October 17, 1908
†June 29, 1941

Career as racing driver from 1927 to 1940.
Began his career in 1927 racing motorbikes. He was a junior driver in the Mercedes-Benz racing team from 1936 to 1939. Won the 1940 Mille Miglia riding a BMW together with Huschke von Hanstein. He died in a motoring accident

1954/55

JUAN MANUEL FANGIO (ARG)
*June 24, 1911
†July 17, 1995

Career as racing driver from 1934 to 1958.
First drove for Mercedes-Benz in a W154 in 1951 in Argentina, went on to win a total of five World Champion titles, of which two were back-to-back victories in the 1954/55 seasons in the Mercedes-Benz W196

KARL KLING (D)
*September 16, 1910

Career as racing driver from 1947 to 1961.
Three times German Champion in a Veritas. Works driver with Daimler-Benz from 1950. Took first place in the Carrera Panamericana and finished second in the 1952 Mille Miglia – on each occasion with Hans Klenk

HANS HERRMANN (D)
*February 23, 1928

Career as racing driver from 1952 to 1970.
Joined Daimler-Benz as a junior driver in 1954, though left the Mercedes team after an accident in Monaco in 1955. He ended his career with a win driving a Porsche at Le Mans in 1970

STIRLING MOSS (GB)
*September 17, 1929

Career as racing driver from 1948 to 1962.
Joined Mercedes-Benz as a works driver in 1955. Secured the World Championships title in sports car racing that year with three wins in his Mercedes 300 SLR – the Mille Miglia, Tourist Trophy and the Targa Florio

PIERO TARUFFI (I)
*October 12, 1906
†January 12, 1988

Career as racing driver from 1923 to 1957 on two and four wheels. In 1955 switched from Scuderia Ferrari to Mercedes-Benz and finished the season with a fourth place in the British Grand Prix and as runner-up in the Italian Grand Prix

ANDRÉ SIMON (F)
*January 5, 1920

Career as racing driver from 1948 to 1965.
Early successes with a Simca-Gordini in 1950, from 1952 with Ferrari. Switched to Mercedes in 1955 after Hans Herrmann's accident and raced both in Formula One and in sports car events

from 1994

ANDREA DE CESARIS (I)
*May 31, 1959

Career as racing driver from 1978 to 1994.
Drove more than 200 Formula One races over 15 years, replacing the injured Karl Wendlinger in the Sauber-Mercedes after the 1994 Monaco Grand Prix

MARK BLUNDELL (GB)
*April 8, 1966

Career as racing driver since 1981. Began with motocross, 1984 Formula Ford 1600, 1987 Formula 3000 and 1991 Formula 1. Replaced Nigel Mansell at McLaren-Mercedes in 1995, secured five points-finishes. Since 1996 Champ Car in the USA

KARL WENDLINGER (A)
*December 20, 1968

Career as racing driver since 1983. Was part of the 1990 junior team driving Sauber-Mercedes Group C sports cars, wins with Jochen Mass and Michael Schumacher. From 1993 entered Formula One with Sauber-Mercedes. Serious accident in Monaco in 1994. Nowadays successfully involved in sports car racing

HEINZ-HARALD FRENTZEN (D)
*May 18, 1967

Career as racing driver since 1980. In 1990 he drove long distance races in the Mercedes-Benz C11, then after three years in Formula 3000 joined Sauber-Mercedes in the 1994 season to drive in Formula One, switching to Jordan in July 2001

NIGEL MANSELL (GB)
*August 8, 1959

Career as racing driver from 1980 to 1995.
World Champion in 1992 in a Williams-Renault and winner of the 1994 CART Championship in the USA. Drove two races for McLaren-Mercedes in 1995

MIKA HAKKINEN (SF)
*September 28, 1968

Career as racing driver since 1980. Six years' apprenticeship in kart racing, then in 1987 won the Finnish, Swedish and Scandinavian titles in Formula Ford 1600. Works driver with McLaren since 1993, World Champion with McLaren-Mercedes in 1998 and 1999

DAVID COULTHARD (GB)
*March 27, 1971

Career as racing driver since 1982. After a period in kart racing, he drove for the Paul Stewart Racing team in junior formula races. Works driver with McLaren-Mercedes since 1996, won his first race for the McLaren-Mercedes team at the 1997 Australian Grand Prix

JAN MAGNUSSON (DK)
*June 4, 1973

Career as racing driver since 1984. Danish Kart Champion 1985/86. Junior Kart World Championships 1987/89, Senior Kart WC 1990, British Formula 3 Championships 1991, starts for AMG-Mercedes in the ITC 1995/96, test driver for McLaren, one start for McLaren-Mercedes in Formula One at Aida (Japan) – finished 10th

SILVER ARROWS –
THE EXTENDED FAMILY

Left-hand page: The most exquisite version of the gullwing Mercedes is the 300 SLR with an 8-cylinder racing engine, used by Rudolf Uhlenhaut as his "company car"

Caracciola's racing limousine sets the ball rolling

The color silver has adorned most Mercedes-Benz sports and racing cars since June 3, 1934. But strict historians regard only the Grand Prix cars as being the true Silver Arrows. This view, whilst preventing an inflation of the Silver Arrows themselves, brings with it the risk of our paying less attention to some of the delightful spin-offs to have come from engineering developments, or even of overlooking altogether some of the most magnificent pieces from earlier periods.

One such sideways move was ventured by the racing department as early as 1934, when a sort of airplane cockpit hood was placed over the driver's seat of the latest W25 racing car. This aerodynamically improved monoposto was immediately nicknamed "the racing limousine", though this failed rather to capture the actual purpose of the car. It had really been designed to allow Rudolf Caracciola to attempt record-breaking runs at Gyon in Hungary and at the Avus circuit. With its 3990 cm³ straight-8 engine producing 398 hp, this uniquely styled vehicle had a top speed of 318 km/h.

The next stage of this development came in 1936 with the enclosed bodywork of the streamlined record-breaking car, whose technical specifications were encoded in the designation W25/MD25DAB.

Readers of earlier chapters will already be acquainted with the abbreviation W25 – the first of all the Silver Arrows, with which Rudolf Caracciola became European Champion in 1935. The rest of the code – MD25DAB – informs the insider that we are not dealing here with the relatively light 8-cylinder in-line type M5 engine developed for the 750-kg formula, but an obviously much more complex piece of machinery. MD25DAB is shorthand for a 12-cylinder engine developed in the 1930s out of

"an addiction to speed"

and a desire to break records. The V12's cylinders were set at an angle of 60 degrees, and with an 82 mm bore and an 88 mm stroke it had a total displacement of 5576 cm³. But at 300 kg it was far too heavy for the lean 750-kg cars. Nevertheless, in its first development stage the engine developed 616 hp. That

For record attempts in 1934 a kind of airplane cockpit hood was fitted to the Grand Prix car

was enough for a quick spin in the W25 at 372 km/h. And when racing permitted cars other than those designed for the Grand Prix formula to take to the circuit, this mighty W25 was always keen to put in an appearance. Because of its heavy engine and various modifications, the racing monster tipped the scales not at 750 kg excluding fluids and tires, but at a race-ready 1216 kg.

"The W25, the most powerful"

of the so-called formule libre racing cars to line up on the Avus near Berlin on May 30, 1937, had in the meantime had its 12-cylinder engine and two Roots blowers tweaked to deliver 756 hp. The extent to which Mercedes-Benz had rattled the beast's cage in preparation for Europe's fastest race is documented by the maximum speeds this W25 achieved in each of its gears: 156 km/h in first, 243 km/h in second, 275 km/h in third, and 370 km/h in fourth gear. Manfred von Brauchitsch was fearless enough to set a new lap record, pushing the mighty racing leviathan to an incredible average speed of 278 km/h and finishing the race in first place after a restart.

By October 1937 the much more up-to-date running gear of the new W125 racing car was hiding its powerful 5.6-liter 12-cylinder engine under an aerodynamically refined aluminum casing. In pursuit of new

Silver Arrows – the extended family

The "racing limousine" was capable of reaching 318 km/h as well as dangerously high temperatures in the cockpit

world records, this time on the autobahn between Frankfurt and Darmstadt on October 28, Caracciola reached 397 km/h. Exactly three months later, on January 28, 1938, the Mercedes-Benz record team returned to the same stretch of motorway, still used today as the A3 motorway. For the occasion, the W125 had been fitted with a new bodyshell, courtesy of the German Aviation Research Institute in Berlin-Adlershof, which reduced the aerodynamic drag coefficient to just 0.157. This time the 12-cylinder powered the record-breaking car to an impressive 432.3 km/h, and with that Caracciola reached a speed which would never be surpassed on normal roads.

In addition to this record-breaking ultra high-speed car, ironed-flat for aerodynamic effect, the racing department at Mercedes-Benz also came up with a more curvaceous design in the late 1930s, which had the considerably smaller front profile of just 1.67 m² and the slightly higher drag coefficient of 0.184.

Beneath this body was the engineering of the W154 3-liter car and its smaller 12-cylinder engine, capable of almost 500 hp when chasing speed records. The record-breaking attempts took place on a purpose-built stretch of what is today the A9 motorway near Dessau. Timed from standstill over one kilometer the car managed an average speed of 177.3 km/h, and 204.5 km/h over the one mile distance.

In 1939 the W125 – banned from the Grand Prix circuits – distinguished itself in other ways. This retired European Champion still packed a mighty punch with its 5.7 liter 8-cylinder engine and 646 hp, and now intended to lay claim to the title

"King of the Mountains"

For what drivers liked best when the going got steep was a powerful engine with lots of torque. In a close-fought duel on the Großglockner, the youthful Hermann Lang and his aging W125 fought off the chal-

Driving the Mercedes W25, with its MD25DAB engine, Manfred von Brauchitsch recorded a lap average on the Avus of 278 km/h. A set of tires lasted just four laps

The record-breaking version of the W25 succeeded in getting close to the 400-km/h barrier in 1937, but even with an available 736 hp the elusive mark remained just out of reach

lenge of Hans Stuck in his 16-cylinder Auto Union to take the title European Hillclimb Champion of 1939.

The first Silver Arrows of the post-war era are much more modest in their display of power. When the decision was made in 1951 to build a sports car with a view to returning the following year to the lively world of post-war racing, the first variants of the Mercedes Benz 300 SL were the results. The early racing version is a convincing prototype of the later series model. An unmistakable feature was the inclusion even then of the legendary gullwing doors.

But the racing department had to rely on series assemblies where the engine was concerned. Although the Mercedes 300, the "Adenauer", was once again able to lend its 3-liter 6-cylinder engine, this was only able to manage a modest 115 hp in its early years. Even after a complete make-over, the engine struggled to maintain a reliable 171 hp. Alfred Neubauer was less than pleased at the paltry results and had little faith in Rudolf Uhlenhaut's bold project. Uhlenhaut, however, wanted nothing more than to build racing cars again, and the talented engineer had evidently succeeded in convincing Neubauer and the management team that by using

"intelligent engineering"

Mercedes-Benz was capable of securing victory against high performance challengers.

With the first version of the 300 SL, the strange situation arose that the racing version's 3-liter 6-cylinder in-line engine with carburetors and 171 hp was far less powerful than the 1954 model, on sale in the dealerships, with direct injection and 210 hp.

But Uhlenhaut's racing sports cars were light, aerodynamic and very efficient. They soon proved that in engineering terms they were on the right track.

At Monza in March 1938, Mercedes-Benz carried out tests on an aerodynamic version of the Grand Prix car, modelled along the lines of the record-breaking car

Silver Arrows – the extended family

The curvaceous record-breaking version of the Mercedes W154 was used for record attempts from a standing start. It covered the kilometer from standstill in 20.3 seconds with an average speed of 177.3 km/h

The team of Karl Kling and Hans Klenk started the season in May with a very convincing performance in the Mille Miglia in Italy. From Brescia to Rome they held a narrow lead ahead of Giovanni Bracco in the much more powerful Ferrari 250, but then lost six minutes at a pit stop because one of the knock-off wheel nuts would not release. Nevertheless they reached the finished in Brescia in second place.

In June the same year at the 24-hour Le Mans race, the Mercedes-Benz 300 SL faced competitors with much greater firepower – especially since output on the Mercedes had been cut to 166 hp to improve endurance. This call for stamina brought the hoped-for success: Hermann Lang and Fritz Riess finished the race in first place.

There was always plenty of action along the route of the Carrera Panamericana in Mexico

The streamlined body of the 432 km/h record-breaking car encased an ice box in the place of a radiator and boasted a drag coefficient of just 0.181

A third unforgettable victory in the Mercedes-Benz 300 SL was achieved by Karl Kling and Hans Klenk in November 1952, when they won the Carrera Panamericana in Mexico. A large slice of the credit for the successes in Italy and Mexico was due to

"navigator Hans Klenk",

whose pace notes not only recorded all bends and correct approach speeds, but also warnings of any spots where danger may be lurking. Klenk's book became the model for all rally "prayer books", but one thing it failed to predict was the vulture which crashed through the navigator's windscreen. That evening after the stage was over, Hans' misfortune was the subject of much conversation. The navigator insisted on having metal bars mounted to protect the 300 SL's new windscreen.

A Silver Arrow with a quite different character was the Mercedes 300 SLR of 1955, a racing sports car very much in the style of the series production model. But appearances can be deceptive, for beneath the elegant lines of the aluminum shell there thundered the entire race technology of a Grand Prix car.

The straight-8 racing engine differed in one significant detail, however. Instead of the normal 2.5 liters, it had a full 3-liter displacement. Although this brought only a minimal increase in output from 290 to 300 hp, the lower compression ratio meant that the larger engine could run on normal super gasoline.

This was the car in which Stirling Moss and Denis Jenkinson completed the Mille Miglia in May 1955 in the never-bettered time of 10 hours, 7 minutes and 48 seconds. Here too, Jenkinson contributed solid support to the win by communicating instructions despite the roaring headwind using prearranged hand signals. In its one and only active season, the Mercedes-Benz 300 SLR finished triumphant. When Moss and Peter Collins finished first ahead of teammates Fangio and Kling in the Targa Florio late in the year, Mercedes-Benz clinched the Sports Car World Championships. At the Le Mans 24-hour race in 1955, the Mercedes 300 SLR Roadster made its first and only appearance with a parachute-like air brake. This had been the subject of experimentation back in 1952,

for at a time when racing drivers often had to decelerate from speeds of 300 km/h using four drum brakes, they were thankful for any support they could get – even if the contribution to overall braking was a relatively modest 1.8 m/s^2.

The second appearance of the Mercedes-Benz works team at Le Mans ended in tragedy, the consequence of which was a cessation of motor racing activities. Through no fault of his own, the Mercedes driver Pierre Levegh ploughed into one of the stands in his 300 SLR, killing 81 spectators. With that, Mercedes' involvement in the race was over, and at the end of the season the team announced a complete withdrawal from motor sport for a lengthy period.

This came as a particularly bitter blow to the man who had literally engineered the team's success, Rudolf Uhlenhaut – his cherished "company car" providing a crumb of consolation, perhaps. This quite remarkable coupe, dreamt up by Uhlenhaut himself, had a body which synthesized the timeless beauty of the series production model with the more aggressive lines of the open racing version. And, of course, at his behest, the sleek bodyshell housed that thoroughbred racing engine. That a few horsepower may have been lost along the way – the result of efforts to tone down the engine's rather loud behavior – detracted little from the fact that Uhlenhaut was able to spend the

In 1955 the Mercedes 300 SLR roadsters were still without disk brakes, but they made use of a parachute-like flip-up air brake

rest of his life driving one of the fastest sports cars ever to take to German roads. His personal car clocked a top speed of 272 km/h against a stopwatch.

After a very long interlude, the Silver Arrows story eventually resumed again in the 1980s with sports cars of a closed design. On his long road to the top in Formula One, the Swiss race team manager Peter Sauber had arrived at the large Group C sports cars by the mid-1980s. He experimented with engines supplied by Ford and BMW, but with these success eluded him.

As a result Sauber entered into discussion with Mercedes-Benz, and before long the two came up with an engine which, although no spring chicken, could still pack a punch. With this unit a Mercedes C111/IV had set new world records back in 1979 on the Italian circular track at Nardo, covering the 100 km distance in 22 minutes and 32 seconds – equivalent to an

The start number 722 on the winning car of the 1955 Mille Miglia refers to its 7.22 a.m. start time in Brescia

"average speed of 375.670 km/h".

The basis of this powerhouse was a series production M 117 engine, a relatively conventional V8 unit with a cast iron block and one overhead camshaft per aluminum cylinder head operating the two valves per cylinder. When fitted inside the Mercedes-Benz 450 SE this engine was not particularly powerful by today's standards – its displacement of 4520 cm^3 developed just 225 hp.

In the record-breaking version the bore was increased to 4820 cm^3 and boost was supplied by two turbochargers, achieving 500 hp at 6200 rpm and a maximum torque of 599 Newton meters at 5250 rpm. Seven years later the same design of engine was installed in the Sauber C8, though this time with 4973 cm^3 displacement and a considerably higher output – 700 hp at 7000 rpm and 800 Newton meters at 5500 rpm.

In 1988 Mercedes-Benz made its official return to motor sport, but this was not yet to be the renaissance of the Silver Arrows. Sporting the advertising logos of the Daimler-Benz Group's new subsidiary AEG, the Sauber C9 appeared sporting a new black outfit decorated with the white lines and dots of an electronic circuit board. Racing engine design for the new C9 sports car followed the state of series development. By this time the M 119 had been introduced into series models, a state-of-the-art V8 engine with aluminum block and cylinder heads and with four camshafts and four valves per unit.

This design of a race engine weighing just 212 kg was capable of developing considerable power across a broad range. Under race conditions it was driven with an output of 720 hp at 7000 rpm – good for going the distance and sparing on fuel. When it came down to fastest times in qualifying, however, it could easily be pushed as high as 900 hp by increas-

The Sauber-Mercedes C11 was simply light years ahead of the competition in the years 1989/90, winning 16 out of the 18 races it took part in

The chance to ride pillion in the tandem version of the McLaren-Mercedes Formula One race car provides a few privileged guests with the experience of a lifetime

ing the boost pressure. With reduced boost pressure for race conditions, torque rose to 810 Newton meters, but engine speed dropped to 3500 rpm.

From 1989 onwards, the new Sauber-Mercedes color was a gleaming classic silver. As a form of tribute, the team celebrated with a

"victory at Le Mans"

and the Sports Car World Championship. The successful C9 survived until 1990 without any need to be replaced. Then, at Peter Sauber's exclusive racing car factory in Hinwil, the C11 was born – the earlier aluminum monocoque design having been replaced by one of carbon fiber composite. Interestingly, for linguistic reasons there was no Type C10, since this designation, in its German pronunciation, was a little too close for comfort to the dreaded tsetse fly which spread sleeping sickness throughout the tropics.

In the long Group C races, the C11 with its 730 hp reached speeds of almost 400 km/h on the long straights. The wind tunnel had been used to optimize aerodynamic design of the body shell, guaranteeing also a good downforce. The C11 were simply light years ahead of the competition, taking the world title in 1989/90 and winning 16 out of the 18 races they took part in.

These high speeds gave grounds for concern among the sport's ruling bodies, however. For this reason a new regulation was introduced in 1991 which banned turbochargers and restricted displacement to 3.5 liters – the same restrictions also introduced into Formula One.

Consequently this brought to an end the era of large series production engines which derived their power for racing from boost pressure. Mercedes-Benz, in reply, came up with the innovative C291 with its M291 thoroughbred racing engine. For a transmission system intended for racing, the design was rather unusual, since the 12 cylinders lay flat at an angle of 180 degrees to one another. The crankshaft with six

Jean-Louis Schlesser, who was later to head off into the desert to win the Paris–Dakar, became Sports Car World Champion in 1989 and also took the same title with Mauro Baldi

For the 1998/99 season AMG built the CLK-LM, which differed in one significant respect: it now had a 5-liter V8 engine developing over 600 hp. In this car Klaus Ludwig and Ricardo Zonta won the Fiat GT championships

cranks and two connecting rods attached to the crankpin shows the engine to be a V12.

The much smaller naturally aspirated engine was capable of reaching almost the same power output as the large turbo transmission systems, but it needed considerably higher revs – 700 hp at 12,500 rpm. Its torque of 400 Newton meters, on the other hand, was only half as high as during the turbocharger era, and even this figure was achieved only at 9000 rpm.

The Mercedes-Benz C291 struggled through the 1991 season with a string of mechanical failures, the junior team of Schumacher and Wendlinger notching up the only victory. This they did on the only occasion the new Japanese Autopolis circuit came to international prominence.

More celebrated, perhaps, were those who achieved success with the Sauber-Mercedes: Mauro Baldi, Peter Dumbreck, Heinz-Harald Frentzen, Jochen Mass, Henry Pescarolo, Manuel Reutter, Michael Schumacher and Karl Wendlinger.

At the end of the season, when Peter Sauber's Formula One project marked the beginning of a new chapter, Mercedes-Benz withdrew for a while from sports car racing.

By 1998 and 1999, however, the silver-colored Mercedes AMG CLK-GTR and the CLK-LM were back in competition. During their last GT involvement, Mercedes made the uncomfortable discovery that race conditions were not always as predictable as those in the wind tunnel. The young British driver Peter Dumbreck was to find this out at first hand during the 24-hour Le Mans race. In the turbulent air thrown up behind one of his opponents, his car reared up, took off and flew into the woods bordering the track. Although Dumbreck was able to walk clear of the wreckage, this spelled the end not just for Mercedes' participation in the 24-hour Le Mans, but also for all further GT events.

A joint venture with AMG in 1998 gave rise to a racing sports car which borrowed stylistically from the Mercedes SLK. The CLK-GTR has a 6-liter V12 engine producing 600 hp

TECHNICAL DATA

MERCEDES W25

ENGINE
Eight-cylinder in-line, twin overhead camshafts, four valves per cylinder, single Roots compressor

M 25 A 1934
Bore 78 mm, stroke 88 mm, displacement 3360 cm^3, compression ratio 7.5, boost pressure 0.66 bar, output 260 kW (354 hp) at 5800 rpm, max. torque 422 Nm at 3000 rpm, engine weight 203 kg

M 25 C 1935
Bore 82 mm, stroke 102 mm, displacement 4310 cm^3, compression ratio 7.3, boost pressure 0.66 bar, output 296 kW (402 hp) at 5800 rpm, max. torque 500 Nm at 3000 rpm, engine weight 206 kg

M 25 E 1936
Bore 86 mm, stroke 102 mm, displacement 4740 cm^3, compression ratio 8.0, boost pressure 1.11 bar, output 333 kW (453 hp) at 5800 rpm, max. torque 631 Nm at 3000 rpm, engine weight 211 kg

All engines with dry sump lubrication

TRANSMISSION
Single-plate dry clutch, four-speed transmission, differential with lock, rear axle drive

RUNNING GEAR
U-section pressed steel frame, front axle with double wishbones, coil springs, rear axle with two transverse links and pull rods (swing axle), leaf springs, front and rear friction dampers

BRAKES
Four hydraulically-operated drum brakes

TIRES
front 5.25 x 17, rear 5.25 x 19

DIMENSIONS AND WEIGHTS
Wheelbase 2725 mm (2460 mm "Kurzer Wagen" short version 1936), length x width x height 4040 x 1771 x 1160 mm, unladen weight excluding fluids and tires 750 kg, race-ready weight excluding fuel and driver 847 kg, tank capacity 215 liters

TOP SPEED
with longest gear ratios 300 km/h

FUEL CONSUMPTION
84–100 l/100 km

Mercedes W25

MERCEDES W125

ENGINE
Grand Prix engine
Eight-cylinder in-line engine, twin overhead camshafts, four valves per cylinder, Roots compressor, bore 94 mm, stroke 102 mm, displacement 5660 cm^3, compression ratio 8.9, boost pressure 0.86 bar, output 423 kW (575 hp) at 5500 rpm, max. torque 926 Nm at 3000 rpm, engine weight 223 kg, dry sump lubrication

Hill-climb engine
Eight-cylinder in-line engine, twin overhead camshafts, four valves per cylinder, Roots compressor, bore 94 mm, Stroke 102 mm, displacement 5660 cm^3, compression 8.9, boost pressure 0,95 bar, output 475 kW (646 hp) at 5800 rpm, max. torque 964 Nm at 3000 rpm, engine weight 225 kg, dry sump lubrication

TRANSMISSION
Single-plate dry clutch, four-speed transmission, differential with lock, rear axle drive

RUNNING GEAR
Frame of oval-section tubing with four cross-members, front axle with double wishbones, coil springs and friction dampers, De Dion rear axle (swing axle), leaf springs and friction dampers

BRAKES
Four hydraulically-operated drum brakes

TIRES
front 5.25 x 19, rear 7.00 x 22

DIMENSIONS AND WEIGHTS
Wheelbase 2798 mm, length x width x height 4040 x 1771 x 1160 mm, unladen weight excluding fluids and tires 750 kg, race-ready weight excluding fuel and driver 847 kg, tank capacity 215 liters

TOP SPEED
with longest gear ratios 300 km/h

FUEL CONSUMPTION
84–98 l/100 km

Mercedes W165

MERCEDES W154

ENGINE
M 154
V12 with 60 degree cylinder angle, two overhead camshafts per bank, four valves per cylinder, two Roots-type compressors,
bore 67 mm, stroke 70 mm,
displacement 2962 cm³, compression ratio 6.0, boost pressure 1.38 bar,
output 333 kW (453 hp) at 8000 rpm,
max. torque 441 Nm at 5000 rpm,
engine weight 254 kg,
dry sump lubrication

M 163
V12 with 60 degree cylinder angle, two overhead camshafts per bank, four valves per cylinder, one two-stage Roots-type compressor,
bore 67 mm, stroke 70 mm,
displacement 2962 cm³, compression ratio 7.2, boost pressure 1.31 bar,
output 344 kW (480 hp) at 7500 rpm,
max. torque 490 Nm at 5500 rpm,
engine weight 274 kg,
dry sump lubrication

TRANSMISSION
Single-plate dry clutch, four-speed transmission, differential with lock, rear axle drive

RUNNING GEAR
Frame of oval-section tubing with four cross-members, front axle with double wishbones, coil springs, De Dion rear axle with longitudinal control arms and torsion bar dampers, front and rear hydraulic dampers

BRAKES
Four hydraulically-operated drum brakes

TIRES
front 5.50 x 19, rear 7.00 x 19,
over 225 km/h front 6.50 x 19, rear 7.00 x 22

DIMENSIONS AND WEIGHTS
Wheelbase 2210 mm,
length x width x height
4250 x 1750 x 1040 mm,
race-ready weight excluding fuel and driver 981 kg,
tank capacity ca. 390 liters

TOP SPEED
with longest gear ratios
330 km/h

FUEL CONSUMPTION
180 l/100 km

MERCEDES W165

ENGINE
V8 engine with 90 degree cylinder angle, two overhead camshafts per bank, four valves per cylinder, two Roots-type compressors,
bore 64 mm, stroke 58 mm,
displacement 1495 cm³, compression ratio 7.0, boost pressure 1.38 bar,
output 181 kW (246 hp) at 7500 rpm,
max. torque 241 Nm at 6000 rpm,
engine weight 190 kg,
dry sump lubrication

TRANSMISSION
Single-plate dry clutch, five-speed transmission, differential with lock, rear axle drive

RUNNING GEAR
Frame of oval-section tubing with four cross-members, front axle with double wishbones, coil springs, De Dion rear axle with longitudinal control arm and torsion bar dampers, front and rear hydraulic dampers

BRAKES
Four hydraulically-operated drum brakes

TIRES
front 5 x 17, rear 6 x 17

DIMENSIONS AND WEIGHTS
Wheelbase 2450 mm,
length x width x height
3860 x 1510 x 850 mm,
race-ready weight excluding fuel and driver 718 kg,
tank capacity 250 liters

TOP SPEED
with longest gear ratios
274 km/h

FUEL CONSUMPTION
137 l/100 km

Mercedes W154

MERCEDES W196 "Streamlined" 1954

ENGINE
M 196/1954
Eight-cylinder in-line engine, canted at 53 degrees, twin overhead camshafts, two valves per cylinder, desmodromic valve control,
bore 76 mm, stroke 68.8 mm, displacement 2498 cm^3, compression ratio 7.5, output 188 kW (256 hp) at 8250 rpm,
max. torque 256 Nm at 6450 rpm, dry sump lubrication

TRANSMISSION
Single-plate dry clutch, five-speed transmission, differential with lock, rear axle drive

RUNNING GEAR
Tubular steel space frame, front axle with double wishbones, coil springs, single-joint swing axle with longitudinal control arm and coil springs, hydraulic telescopic dampers front and rear

BRAKES
Four hydraulically-operated drum brakes

TIRES
front 6.00 x 16, rear 7.00 x 16

DIMENSIONS AND WEIGHTS
Wheelbase 2350 mm,
length x width x height
4360 x 1680 x 1020 mm,
race-ready weight excluding fuel and driver 829 kg,
tank capacity 265 liters

TOP SPEED
with longest gear ratios
300 km/h

FUEL CONSUMPTION
30 - 40 l/100 km

MERCEDES W196 "Monoposto" 1954

ENGINE
M 196/1954
Eight-cylinder in-line engine, canted at 53 degrees, twin overhead camshafts, two valves per cylinder, desmodromic valve control,
bore 76 mm, stroke 68.8 mm, displacement 2498 cm^3, compression ratio 7.5, output 188 kW (256 hp) at 8250 rpm,
max. torque 256 Nm at 6250 rpm,
engine weight 265 kg,
dry sump lubrication

TRANSMISSION
Single-plate dry clutch, five-speed transmission, differential with lock, rear axle drive

RUNNING GEAR
Tubular steel space frame, front axle with double wishbones, coil springs, single-joint swing axle with longitudinal control arm and coil springs, hydraulic telescopic dampers front and rear

BRAKES
Four hydraulically-operated drum brakes

TIRES
front 6.00 x 16, rear 7.00 x 16

DIMENSIONS AND WEIGHTS
Wheelbase 2200 mm,
length x width x height
4250 x 1625 x 1010 mm,
race-ready weight excluding fuel and driver 729 kg,
tank capacity 265 liters

TOP SPEED
with longest gear ratios
300 km/h

FUEL CONSUMPTION
30 – 40 l/100 km

Mercedes W196 "Streamlined"

MERCEDES W196 "Monoposto" 1955

ENGINE
M 196/1955
Eight-cylinder in-line engine, canted at 53 degrees, twin overhead camshafts, two valves per cylinder, desmodromic valve control,
bore 76 mm, stroke 68.8 mm, displacement 2498 cm³, compression ratio 7.5, output 213 kW (310 hp) at 8500 rpm, max. torque 256 Nm at 6450 rpm,
engine weight 290 kg,
dry sump lubrication

TRANSMISSION
Single-plate dry clutch, five-speed transmission, differential with lock, rear axle drive

RUNNING GEAR
Tubular steel space frame, front axle with double wishbones, coil springs, single-joint swing axle with longitudinal control arm and coil springs, hydraulic telescopic dampers front and rear

BRAKES
Four hydraulically-operated drum brakes

TIRES
front 6.00 x 16, rear 7.00 x 16

DIMENSIONS AND WEIGHTS
Wheelbase 2150 mm,
length x width x height
4250 x 1625 x 1010 mm,
race-ready weight excluding fuel and driver 640 kg,
tank capacity 265 liters

TOP SPEED
with Monaco gear ratios
241 km/h

FUEL CONSUMPTION
30-40 l/100 km

MERCEDES W196 "Streamlined" 1955

ENGINE
M 196/1955
Eight-cylinder in-line engine, canted at 53 degrees, twin overhead camshafts, two valves per cylinder, desmodromic valve control,
bore 76 mm, stroke 68.8 mm, displacement 2498 cm³, compression ratio 7.5, output 213 kW (310 hp) at 8500 rpm, max. torque 256 Nm at 6450 rpm,
engine weight 290 kg,
dry sump lubrication

TRANSMISSION
Single-plate dry clutch, five-speed transmission, differential with lock, rear axle drive

RUNNING GEAR
Tubular steel space frame, front axle with double wishbones, coil springs, single-joint swing axle with longitudinal control arm and coil springs, hydraulic telescopic dampers front and rear

BRAKES
Four hydraulically-operated drum brakes

TIRES
front 6.00 x 16, rear 7.00 x 16

DIMENSIONS AND WEIGHTS
Wheelbase 2350 mm,
length x width x height
4360 x 1680 x 1020 mm,
race-ready weight excluding fuel and driver 758 kg,
tank capacity 265 liters

TOP SPEED
with fastest gear ratios
302 km/h

FUEL CONSUMPTION
30-40 l/100 km

Mercedes W196 "Monoposto"

Mercedes W196 "Monoposto"

McLaren-Mercedes MP 4/13

McLAREN-MERCEDES MP 4/10 1995

ENGINE
V10 engine, 75 degree cylinder angle, two overhead camshafts per bank, four valves per cylinder, pneumatic valve dampers, adjustable intake pipe, throttle valve load adjustment, manifold injection,
bore 90 mm, stroke 47.15 mm, displacement 2998 cm^3, compression ratio 12.8, output 514 kW (699 hp) at 15,250 rpm,
max. torque 335 Nm at 12,500 rpm, dry sump lubrication
capacity 8.0 liters,
TAGtronic Electronic Management System,
engine weight 123 kg

TRANSMISSION
Multi-disk carbon clutch, semi-automatic six-speed transmission, differential with lock

RUNNING GEAR
Monocoque made of molded carbon fiber components, servo-assisted rack and pinion steering, double wishbone front and rear, torsion bar/damper system operated by push-rods and rocker arms

BRAKES
Four disk brakes with carbon fiber brake disks

TIRES
front 265/55 x 13, rear 325/45 x 13

BASIC WEIGHT
Wheelbase 2850 mm, track front/rear 1690/1605 mm, width 2000 mm

Weight including driver 595 kg

McLAREN-MERCEDES MP 4/11 1996

ENGINE
V10 engine, 75 degree cylinder angle, two overhead camshafts per bank, four valves per cylinder, pneumatic valve dampers, adjustable intake pipe, rotary slide load-adjustment, manifold injection,
bore 89 mm, stroke 48,22 mm, displacement 2998 cm^3, compression ratio 12.8, output 538 kW (741 hp) at 15,750 rpm,
max. torque 355 Nm at 13,000 rpm, dry sump lubrication
capacity 8.0 liters,
TAGtronic Electronic Management System,
engine weight 123 kg

TRANSMISSION
Multi-disk carbon clutch, semi-automatic six-speed transmission, differential with lock

RUNNING GEAR
Monocoque made of molded carbon fiber components, servo-assisted rack and pinion steering, double wishbone front and rear, torsion bar/damper system operated by push-rods and rocker arms

BRAKES
Four disk brakes with carbon fiber brake disks

TIRES
front 265/55 x 13, rear 325/45 x 13

BASIC WEIGHT
width 2000 mm, otherwise no fixed data

Weight including driver 595 kg

McLaren-Mercedes MP 4/13

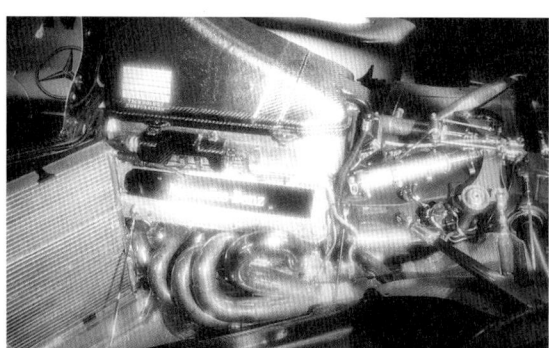

McLAREN-MERCEDES MP 4/12 1997

ENGINE
V10 engine, 72 degree cylinder angle, two overhead camshafts per bank, four valves per cylinder, pneumatic valve dampers, adjustable intake pipe, rotary slide load-adjustment, manifold injection,
displacement 2998 cm^3, all other engine data are confidential,
TAGtronic Electronic Management System

TRANSMISSION
Multi-disk carbon clutch, semi-automatic seven-speed transmission, differential with lock

RUNNING GEAR
Monocoque made of molded carbon fiber components, servo-assisted rack and pinion steering, double wishbone front and rear, torsion bar/damper system operated by push-rods and rocker arms

BRAKES
Four disk brakes with carbon fiber brake disks

TIRES
front 265/55 x 13, rear 325/45 x 13

BASIC WEIGHT
No fixed data,
width restriction 2000 mm

Weight including driver 595 kg

McLAREN-MERCEDES MP 4/13 1998

ENGINE
V10 engine, 72 degree cylinder angle, two overhead camshafts per bank, four valves per cylinder, pneumatic valve dampers, adjustable intake pipe, rotary slide load-adjustment, manifold injection,
displacement 2998 cm^3, all other engine data are confidential,
TAGtronic Electronic Management System

TRANSMISSION
Multi-disk carbon clutch, semi-automatic seven-speed transmission, differential with lock

RUNNING GEAR
Monocoque made of molded carbon fiber components, servo-assisted rack and pinion steering, double wishbone front and rear, torsion bar/damper system operated by push-rods and rocker arms

BRAKES
Four disk brakes with carbon fiber brake disks

TIRES
Regulation grooved tires, 12 ins (305 mm) min. width (front) and 14 ins (355.6 mm) min. width (rear), maximum permitted width 15 ins (380 mm)

BASIC WEIGHT
No fixed data, width restricted to 1800 mm

Weight including driver 600 kg

McLAREN-MERCEDES MP 4/14 1999

ENGINE
V10 engine, 72 degree cylinder angle, two overhead camshafts per bank, four valves per cylinder, pneumatic valve dampers, adjustable intake pipe, rotary slide load-adjustment, manifold injection,
displacement 2998 cm^3, all other engine data are confidential,
TAGtronic Electronic Management System

TRANSMISSION
Multi-disk carbon clutch, semi-automatic seven-speed transmission, differential with lock

RUNNING GEAR
Monocoque made of molded carbon fiber components, servo-assisted rack and pinion steering, double wishbone front and rear, torsion bar/damper system operated by push-rods and rocker arms

BRAKES
Four disk brakes with carbon fiber brake disks

TIRES
Regulation grooved tires, 12 ins (305 mm) min. width (front) and 14 ins (355.6 mm) min. width (rear), maximum permitted width 15 ins (380 mm)

BASIC WEIGHT
No fixed data, width restricted to 1800 mm

Weight including driver 600 kg

All engine data appearing in other publications are deemed by Ilmor to be inaccurate estimates. For this reason we have not made use of these sources.

McLaren-Mercedes

PICTURE CREDITS

SOURCE	PAGE NUMBER
DaimlerChrysler Group Archive	8, 24-29, 30 bottom, 31-45, 60-65, 76-95, 106-111, 146, 148 top, 149 top, 150, 151 bottom, 152, 153 bottom, 154-157, 159, 160-163, 165-167
Daniel Reinhard, Switzerland	124, 135, 137 bottom, 138, 139, 140
Wolfgang Wilhelm, Neustadt/Weinstraße	125-129, 134, 136, 137 top, 141-145, 147, 148 bottom, 149 bottom, 151 top, 153 top
The Wilkins Family Archive, England	30 top
Mario Illien/Ilmor	130-133

All other pictures by Markus Bolsinger